Abiding Light

Praise for *Abiding Light*

If you are navigating an excruciating and unexpected loss, this book is for you. Heidi holds nothing back as she vulnerably shares her intimate journey of grief after losing a loved one to suicide. With perspectives given from multiple family members, her words are sure to aid as a resounding reminder that you are not alone as you grapple with how to move forward.

Rebekah Lyons
Author, *Rhythms of Renewal* and *You Are Free*

Suicide is always a stone unexpectedly dropped in a family's life, creating ripples that linger long after. Heidi Paulec knows this firsthand. In her book, *Abiding Light: In the Shadow of Your Absence*, Heidi writes as a witness, chronicling with honesty and hope her family's grief, and this includes her own. The scar of her beloved cousin's suicide remains tender to this day, but she has seen glimpses of the good—as she writes, "grace amidst the grief." Her words are a gift.

John Blase
Poet and author, *The Jubilee: Poems*

"What could we have done to help?"

In the wake of a loved one's suicide, this unanswerable question weighs heavily on the grieving hearts left behind. Jamie Plinsky, Heidi's "twin" cousin, took his own life at the age of seventeen. Inseparable for most of their formative years, Jamie and Heidi enjoyed an inarticulable bond, a knowing and transcendent relationship that entailed exploration, discovery, the safety of a loving family clan, and mud pies, emerging from the wind-swept grain fields of their Wyoming homestead.

This sort of thing isn't supposed to happen to these sorts of salt-of-the-earth, God-fearing people. Those of us living the mostly fragmented and frenetic lives of modern America would rather idealize such faraway places as somehow remaining untouched by the darkness and hopelessness we sense beneath the surface of the daily grind.

Heidi Paulec's *Abiding Light: In the Shadow of Your Absence* details the vast array of responses from "suicide survivors" through the stories of four generations of family members, immediate and extended, struggling to make sense of a seemingly senseless death. Everyone responds to it differently, of course, ranging from panic to numbness, obsession to suppression, shame to blame. Some experience all of these and more. Others feel only a few.

Heidi is not content, however, to leave us with the long grief that accompanies these survivors (herself included). Each story breaks out of the trauma in its own way—floods of memories that volley back and forth from paralyzing shock to faith. And God's providential and loving care weaves through every retelling of that dreadful January night in 1992. The shadow of absence becomes the shelter of the Almighty.

This is a book that both survivors and those who love those survivors will want to read. Kindness and self-kindness, an awareness of our common humanity, and mindfulness are needed now more than ever, not least in the face of suicide. Embodying a loving, connected presence to ourselves and others by the power of God's Spirit is the only lasting way out of such an abyss. I am grateful to Heidi for helping us to see that the victory of the resurrected Christ is the true center of this story—indeed, "our hope is built on nothing less."

Christopher John Donato
Director of marketing and communication, Trinity International University
Former senior associate editor, *Tabletalk Magazine*
Editor, *Perspectives on the Sabbath*

All of us will have to walk through "The Valley of the Shadow of Death." Some will make that agonizing journey more than once in a lifetime. Using a unique, engaging format, Heidi Paulec recalls how the suicide of a young man and the chill of the shadow impacted her, his family, and relatives. You will gain insights in this book that will help you navigate your own journey, help you comfort people who are in the midst of the shadow, and perhaps insights that can save a life. Most important, you will see that even in the depths of the shadow there is the light of hope if you will lift your eyes to see it.

Ken Davis
Author, *Fully Alive* and speaker

How does death by suicide affect a tight-knit family? Heidi's personal reflections and oral histories from four generations of family bring light to places families so often keep shrouded in darkness. Her poignant writing helps not only to answer questions surrounding one family's experience but shows us gospel hope is never buried, and even in tragedy, God is breathing new life in the stillness.

Lisa Appelo
Widow and single mom to 7
Speaker, Bible teacher, and writer at LisaAppelo.com
Author, *Countdown to Christmas: Unwrap the Real Christmas Story with Your Family in 15 Days*

When the deepest sorrows of life come our way, the voice of empathy and compassion is invaluable. For while no one can say they know precisely how we feel, or just exactly how such darkness is to be navigated, the knowledge that others have traveled a similar path before us can give courage and meaning in the midst of it.

Heidi's voice, and the voices of her family members, provide just that kind of empathetic companionship. Their honest reflections, thoughtfully and artfully collected by Heidi, are evidence that human pain can be endured when walking alongside others we love. This work promises to be a gift to anyone who knows the searing pain of loss that makes no earthly sense, for it draws that reader's attention to the presence of Christ in the midst of it, and the hope that is available to those who wait and watch for it.

Tracy Balzer
Author, *Permission to Ponder: Contemplative Wisdom for the Spiritually Distracted,* Director of Christian Formation, John Brown University

All I can say is Heidi has written something I couldn't look away from, despite my trepidation about the subject matter. This book approaches the exquisite pain of suicide with such poignancy that I felt privileged, as if I'd been invited into the sacred family circle to know each member, and to know Jamie. I'm so thankful Heidi doesn't waste a word on pious cliches but walks barefooted right into the shadowy experience of human shock and loss. Her storytelling rings deeply true, and because of that, so do her words of hope and light. I see this book as a compassionate portrait of familial love tied inevitably to our individual suffering.

Christa Wells
Songwriter

A generation ago, Eric Clapton asked if there would be "Tears in Heaven." Living with the unexpected death of his young son, the artful, poetic song captures the heartache of anyone who has lost someone who was dearly loved. The pain is profound because it cannot not be, and there are no cheap answers.

In this tender story of a family's response to suicide, we listen to the generations who together mourn the death of great-grandson, grandson, son, brother, and cousin, each one deeply wounded, each one differently affected. The gifted guide through this pilgrimage of pain is Heidi Paulec, and this is her family's story of great hope that became great heartache. A tender tale for the heartbroken, yes, but also for those who long for healing, for an honest hint of hope.

Steven Garber

Author, *The Seamless Life: Weaving Together Love and Learning, Worship and Work* , Senior fellow for vocation and the common good, M.J. Murdock Charitable Trust

"Carrying grief is often a heavy work, a sharing work, a work my human pride would prefer be perfected behind closed doors in the dark. But as we hear the cries, enter the prayers, and raise banners of hope, we encourage and endure a faith building together."

More than a memoir, *Abiding Light: In the Shadow of Your Absence* is an invitation to an intimate gathering where grief and hope dance in concentric circles of familiarity. Heidi Paulec thoughtfully writes about the depths of sorrow, the corridors of questioning, and the longing for answers that may never be found even as God redeems and restores. The stories in the book are cut like gemstones as family members spanning four generations reflect on the impact of suicide. There is no attempt to distill pain into a palatable problem to be quickly resolved. Rather, every page offers a refuge for those who, like Paulec, have learned that grief tenderly finds a place to call home in the collective hearts of all who have suffered loss.

Ronne Rock

Author, *One Woman Can Change the World: Reclaiming Your God-Designed Influence and Impact Right Where You Are*

Heidi L. Paulec

Discovering Hope After Sudden Death

ABIDING LIGHT

In the Shadow of Your Absence

NASHVILLE

NEW YORK • LONDON • MELBOURNE • VANCOUVER

Abiding Light

In the Shadow of Your Absence

Published in New York, New York, by Morgan James Publishing. Morgan James is a trademark of Morgan James, LLC. www.MorganJamesPublishing.com

ISBN 9781631953897 paperback
ISBN 9781631953903 eBook
Library of Congress Control Number: 2020948955

Cover Design by:
Megan Dillon
megan@creativeninjadesigns.com

Interior Design by:
Christopher Kirk
www.GFSstudio.com

Morgan James is a proud partner of Habitat for Humanity Peninsula and Greater Williamsburg. Partners in building since 2006.

Get involved today! Visit
MorganJamesPublishing.com/giving-back

In Memory of
C. Jamie Plinsky
August 26, 1974 – January 18, 1992

For My Family and For Yours
Here's to Living Hope

Table of Contents

acknowledgments

Thank you to my family who entrusted these tender stories to me. Thank you for your vulnerability and patience. Your example and encouragement illuminate His goodness—sun up to sun down.

Thank you to literary professionals, including Josh and Kim Johnson, editing team, who polished and refined without losing the distinct voices, and the Morgan James Publishing Team, including Karen Anderson, who recognized the relevance.

Thank you to generous trail-blazing friends—Chris Donato, Tracy Balzer, Ken Davis, Steven Garber, Ronne Rock, Lisa Appelo, John Blase, Bill Enslen, Christa Wells, and Rebekah Lyons.

Thanks to Micah T. Paulec—proofreading & technical support. Thanks to Isaiah A. Paulec—proofreading with thoughtful feedback. Thanks to Holly Miguel—caring correspondence, crocheting, and calming me along the way.

Thank you to professionals in their field—Gary Curmode, Bill Enslen, Megan Faulkner, Cindi Florit, David Pritz, Susanne Folkers, Donald and Marlis Shamblin—for acknowledging need for growing empathy and compassion.

Special thanks to my kick starters—Bill and Kris Fasbender, Eric and Jodie Frye, Kathy Hundley, Michael and Amy Plinsky, Tim and Karen Plinsky, Carlton Plinsky, Elmer and Holly Miguel, Darrell and Wanda Plinsky, Roy and Gretchen Snowden, Dave and Cindy Paulec, Chet and Sarah Bennetts. This work comes out now because of you.

Thank you:

Cory and Jen, Traci, Chris and Michelle—for helping me find my laugh again and discover deeper delights on this side.

My brave tank—Jodie, Kendra, Mandie, Terri, Michelle, and Nicole—for believing and praying Scripture and gently pressing me past my tears.

Prayer team—some since 2007, thank you for persevering with me. He hears our prayers. Here we are.

Abiding Light launch team—Anywhere this message travels will be thanks to your championing it. Thank you for torch-bearing.

Michael—for providing prayers and wellness accountability along the way.

Mom and Dad—for being my biggest cheerleaders, training me to love sunrises, and teaching me hymns and Scripture at a young age, so when the darkness came ... I kept hearing the songs.

Micah—for your creativity, kindness, and continual encouragement.

Isaiah—for your example of endurance and affirming encouragement along the way.

Mia Ruth—you gave me the gift of presence and grounded me when I didn't know I needed it. Thank you for getting me to dance again.

Alex—you walked through the dark with me. Thank you.

foreword

I first encountered suicide, not unlike Heidi, as a teenager. Nineteen and in the US Navy, I was devastated by the loss of my mother to suicide. I shall never forget that terrible day I was called to my executive officer's cabin.

"I have some bad news for you, Petty Officer Enslen. The Red Cross has sent a message to us: 'Your mother is dead. She has taken her own life.'"

I knew of no resources to assist me on that dark, ten-thousand-mile journey home to my mother's lifeless body. How helpful *Abiding Light: In the Shadow of Your Absence* would have been for me at that time.

In more than twenty-five years as a certified grief therapist working in hospice bereavement care and running suicide survivor groups, I have experienced, witnessed, heard, and read many stories about grief. However, this story is especially compelling. Not only is it creatively written, but Heidi's story has taken half a lifetime to get to where it could even be told. It is the evolution from the day of the terrible shock to the place where one could, "delight in hope's tender, yet mighty eternal embrace."

In readable, staccato sentences, Heidi's words paint pictures of feelings. She is eminently qualified to write this story, not only because of her God-gifted talent of writing, but because she has lived this journey. Jamie was born only seven weeks before Heidi, and they grew up together more like twin siblings than first cousins. His death spurred Heidi to think deeply and sincerely about the spiritual journey from devastation to hope one must go through when confronted by the self-inflicted death of a loved one. It simply must be read by others who follow her in this journey. It should also be read by those whose job it is to attempt helping ones who have experienced the pain of suicide as a survivor.

I have spent my entire working life in the prevention and healing of those left in the wake of self-inflicted death. I have long encouraged Heidi to get this work published because I believe it can be a benefit to many others.

Consider:

- Suicide is the second-leading cause of death for young people and rates continue to increase.

- Suicide took the life of 541 service members across the military's active and reserve components in 2018—the highest number since the Defense Department began collecting the data in 2001 and far more deadly than combat.

- Suicide is the tenth overall cause of death for those over the age of ten in the United States, accounting for 1.4 percent of all deaths. That is the equivalent of 10 jet airliners with 300 persons on board crashing each month!

We have needed this book for a long time. Now you have it.

William (Bill) Enslen, M.Div., LMHC

preface

This is a book I wish we did not need. But if you're holding it in your hands, likely you—or someone close to you—is facing loss. This is tender space. We welcome you. We do not open with statistics, because the numbers are distant when the name of our buried loved one rings close and almost too heavy.

We draw you in close. Four generations of a family—my family—share in the first person how loss to suicide affected them. Each a distinct testimony of humanity and hope. Not merely to hear our stories, but to begin to listen and voice your own. We are not alone in this. You are not alone either.

We do not hold educational authority to inform or to instruct, but we do hold our experience as an offering of encouragement. To lament. To mourn. To heal. Together. To discover compassion afresh. To awaken daily delights ... even in the midst of the deep ache of a loved one's absence.

Despite the hard within these pages, He Who is Hope prevails beyond them. I pray he comforts and carries you.

Based on conversations and research with counselors, educators, first responders, medical professionals, military personnel, pastors, professors, and youth ministers, we offer this as a resource for connection and compassionate conversation.

Imagine a charcuterie board (or even just a bowl of trail mix), a box of tissue, a stack of photos, soft music, and a few quiet evenings meeting together for discussion—whether within book clubs, family counseling, grief groups, or the like. I pray you find a voice or two within these pages with whom you relate. And with whom you can pause and relate to those around you.

Heidi L. Paulec

dusk

T hat day, our epic of hope began ... even as death dawned a shrouding darkness on my family. Not an accident. Not an elderly relative. Not even a fit of rage.

Rather, a seventeen-year-old young man silenced and stilled his own heartbeat.

Summertime in the Late 1970s

Just exiting our toddler years, my cousin Jamie and I already knew we contributed in big ways to the family farm operation. We knew our jobs. We needed to stay outside, stay as clean as possible, pick up sticks in the grass, enter any building or worksite of the farm only upon invitation, and stay within the circle of the homestead. This still left us a dozen acres or so to explore, to invent, and to enter our land of make-believe.

Even in those early years, we scouted the boundary lines closely, often encouraging and taunting each other. One particularly sunny morning early in summer, the adults readily sent us outside. After enough pleas, we convinced someone to grant us permission to wander beyond our customary boundary. An epic adventure, even before we had the vocabulary to call it such.

Dressed in our official play clothes—often coordinated shorts, shirts, socks, and tennis shoes—we took off down the driveway, taking a left toward the mailbox. Unlike city mailboxes, our mailbox stood miles away. So, with our plot and plan—quite akin to treasure hunting—we traversed the gravel road of the Great Plains with great hopes of delivering mail to the happy surprise and wonder of our parents and grandparents.

Anticipating our farm-hardy noontime meal, I'm pretty sure we could hear the family's pride and celebration upon our Pony-Express return. It's probably partly why we ventured a little too far for that spring season and even our own stamina.

Amongst our gravel kicking, I think
Woody Guthrie's "This Land is Your Land"
whistled out our pace.

We jibber-jabbered our way into the Wyoming wind, fully focused on the horizon. The dot of the mailbox. Racing. Skipping. Walking. Looking back now and again to see the home-place growing smaller and smaller behind us. *Can you believe this? We're really going somewhere … all by ourselves.*

Eventually, tiredness set in. Our heads drooped a little, and our gaze set toward our shuffling feet. Then we spotted a glistening cluster of crystallized pebbles reflecting in the rising sun. We imagined we'd stuff our pockets full of these "diamonds," a distracting, brighter treasure than the mail we set out for. But what if we came home with both?

Simultaneously, we spotted the protruding mound of treasure along the southern shoulder of the road, just north of the home-place. We scurried over to inspect it. Leaning over it, we spotted tiny parading trains of black-and-red specks heave-hoeing in and out, in and out of tiny holes in the mound. In our fascination observing their order and occupation, we didn't realize their marching led right up Jamie's legs. An entire ant brigade: "Left. Left. Left, right, left ..."

Suddenly, Jamie screeched as his legs jumped and arms thrashed. Swinging and kicking. Slipping ... and falling into the "diamond" mound. The trains of ants instantly derailed and frenzied.

And I started laughing—yes, laughing.

Kicking to his feet, Jamie paused, both feet planted in the cratered mound, now erupting with ants. He looked up and shot a piercing look of panic at me. I grabbed him and started swatting and swiping. So many of them. As we cleared some away, I saw his skin welting red. Looking toward the home-place, I realized how very far, far away we were. And all alone.

Mysteriously moving from girly giggles to pure panic and lifeguard mode, I ran both of us home. Jamie's tears flowing, skin swelling, I just kept repeating, "You're going to be okay. You're going to be okay. Just run with me. Stay with me. I'll hold your hand. You're going to be okay."

Maybe remembering Watty Piper's "The Little Engine That Could"—"I think I can, I think I can, I think I can ..."—or maybe by a miraculous gust of grace, we arrived at the first house dusty and disheveled. The adults swarmed into take-over duty, rushing Jamie off to a bath.

My breath surfaced, racing. We made it. He really is okay, right? His eyes, screaming panic, played over and over in my young mind.

Sometimes, they still do.

How cruel is it that diamond mounds turn into ravenous anthills?

The 23rd Psalm

We grew up going to the same country church our ancestors built for the gathering of community in worship and service of our Lord Jesus. Every Sunday. We sat still, sang hymns, and gleaned much from older generations. Gritty generations often gathered multiple times a week, even amongst wrangling land and livestock. These people paused together to nourish on Scriptures and nourish one another through prayer and service. I remember the ladies, especially the grandmotherly ones (some widows), teaching spiritual formation by example.

Mrs. Hilda, always smiling from deep within her soul, sent birthday cards in the mail to everyone. Mrs. Susie played the piano with precision. And Mrs. Sherry, the young pastor's wife, loved the babies in the nursery. And our Grandma Phyllis sang and billowed her delight in the choir. No matter the size of choir or quartet, her voice inflated the room. She exuded joy most of the time but most especially when she sang songs.

Grandma Phyllis volunteered to teach our Sunday School class one year. We sang, "Jesus Loves Me This I Know," with her nearly every day anyway. How easy she thought it might be, knowing Jamie and I and just a couple other children our age. The endeavor proved to be a real stretch for her, but resulted in us memorizing the 23rd Psalm.

> *The LORD is my shepherd; I shall not want. He maketh me to lie down in green pastures: he leadeth me beside the still waters. He restoreth my soul: he leadeth me in the paths of righteousness for his name's sake. Yea, though I walk through the valley of the shadow of death, I will fear no evil: for thou art with me; thy rod and thy staff they comfort me. Thou preparest a table before me in the presence of mine enemies: thou anointest my head with oil; my cup runneth over. Surely goodness and mercy shall follow me all the days of my life: and I will dwell in the house of the LORD forever.*
> **Psalms 23:1-6 KJV**

Somehow, "the Lord is my shepherd" came easily to us. We'd witnessed neighboring ranchers care for their herds with profound, diligent
responsibility. We'd seen horses come running at the shake-shake of a
grain bucket. Sheep naturally follow the leader, and we'd seen that, too.

The "I shall not want"? Maybe not so easily. Often, I found myself
wanting everything Jamie had. Sadly, I even envied his birthday coming
before mine every year. Our great-grandparents celebrated Jamie's August
birthday before traveling south for the winter, but they always missed my
October birthday.

"Valley of the shadow of death": how utterly foreign! At some point
along the way, death silenced some older men in our congregation. I
remember an older cowboy gentleman I called Grandpa Claude (though
he was not a blood relative) and Uncle Reuben both died. Their weathered skin, distinguished glasses, and stiffened gait indicated life's naturally
slowing pace. Somehow, their deaths followed a predictable, expected
cycle, one I didn't question. Sadness seeped in for a time, yes. I remember
Aunt Ruth climbing the church steps and sitting alone in her pew. Yet I
found I liked remembering people's lives in the whole, the lives we often
hear about only in the funeral service setting.

Somehow, the dissolving diamond mound and erupting anthill
introduced me to tentacles of the shadow of death as I heard the lies
pelting us: "You're alone!" "You won't make it back!" "This pain? All your
fault! If you hadn't pressed for adventure, Jamie would be fine." Subtle
stabs. Venturing off the homestead unleashed hopes, dreams, plans, fail-
ures, and fears like I had never encountered before that day.

Once we returned, the rattle rested. Jamie, bathed and balmed,
assured me he was fine—sore and tired, but fine. He firmly noted we
should never play in anthills again. In the calm, I finally remembered we
failed to get the mail. He tried to reassure me that someone else probably
already did the job, and he was probably right. But disappointment and
discouragement fueled frustration and fatigue.

Someone quieted us with a snack. However, a haunting, unsettling soul-stirring churned within me. This big, beautiful, bountiful world reflects our creator. We already knew this from our Sunday School classes, and we'd seen plenty of his systems. We'd seen barren fields embrace seeds and grow crops. We'd worked sprinklers, rode along tractor runs and combine courses, and took care of badger invasions.

We'd witnessed the hardy efforts bring in the harvest. Big men. Hat hair. Dusty jeans. Worn boots. Calloused hands. We'd tasted the joy of a profitable season, both in Grandpa Ken's study as he worked figures as well as around the dining table where we gathered to feast and give thanks.

But the anthill incident opened my eyes to an evil I previously relegated to a time long ago, a snake in a garden far, far away. Ant armies illustrated the slithering, organized approach of evil's shadowy tentacles: shiny things, horizons and mining mounds, biting pain, numbing, dimming soul.

Sure, we made it home. That day.

> "The challenges looming on the horizon would test every comfortable assumption of Empire and every fiber of personal faith and courage."
> **Stephen Mansfield**
> *Never Give In: The Extraordinary Character of Winston Churchill*

Mud Pies

On another sunny afternoon about the same age, we found ourselves much closer to home. We nestled on a back porch. Hiding from the wind and sneaking water from the hose to make mud in barren planters, we attempted to pass time.

Grandma Ruth spotted us, and she made sure we had proper garden tools. She also sternly reminded us not to run the water hose. Get what we need, and shut it off. We nodded agreement, and she left us to return to her duties.

As we sat there, the wind whistled around us. Jamie and I unearthed dirt clods along with some decent four-year-old philosophical questions. Why do grown-ups want to know our favorite colors? Why do they make us eat food we don't like? Why is the grown-up world and the child world so segregated? (I liked the kids' table and all. We escaped etiquette training when we sat by ourselves. But listening in on enough adult table conversations made me want to talk, too.) Why do the women work the way they do, and why do the men work the way they do? (Although I often complained about our being tossed outside for hours at a time, I couldn't begin to imagine working anywhere else. I preferred raking out the barn to pushing dust around the house any day.) Why do we dress up for church? And why were we the only kids not allowed to run in or around the church?

As Jamie and I sat grabbing and squeezing, grabbing and squeezing the gritty-sticky goop until dirt darkened under our fingernails, Grandma Ruth approached us again. This time, she brought us each a pie tin. She asked, "Have you two ever made mud pies?" We looked at each other, eyes wide.

This time, adventure was coming to us. Although we were already fairly dirt-smudged at this point, we acknowledged our inexperience and eager readiness to experiment. Grandma Ruth helped us move mud into the tins. She told us after we finished loading and decorating them, we could leave them in the sun to bake.

Jamie smoothed his heap meticulously. I impatiently attempted designs. I wanted mine done first (yes, that competitive). And mine needed to be prettier than his. However, his slices would be airhole-less and much more precise than mine. After a while of watching him smooth and re-smooth, I realized, "I don't even like to eat pie." I liked to smell it. I liked to eat leftover crust baked with cinnamon and sugar. I even enjoyed watching other people eat pie. Grown-ups make faces like children when they eat desserts. I just didn't like to eat it myself. So how could I imagine even pretending to like this mud pie? Was all this just wasted time?

Jamie, on the other hand, enjoyed eating real pie. And he enjoyed this make-believe mess. He questioned, along with me, many things that day—and in many days to come. The goodness of pie, however, was not up for question. We completed our mud pie projects and placed them on a sun-exposed ledge. And waited. And we waited. I touched mine. Baking? No way! It was as wet and gooey as ever. "This isn't working!" I hastily complained. We waited some more.

Finally, we ventured through the wind to Grandma Ruth's house to ask how long they would need to bake. She didn't know. She didn't know!?! A grown-up who suggested mud pie-making in the first place didn't know the time they needed to solidify? She suggested going inside to clean up and check later. Jamie acquiesced to the suggestion, while I complained the whole way back to the big house. We were not even school age.

> "Deep within every human heart throbs the undying hope that somebody or something will bring both an explanation of what life is all about and a way to retain the wonder."
> **Ravi Zacharias**
> *Recapture the Wonder*

"He Stopped Laughing"

I sat alone on the fading brown-and-orange sofa as the film projector portrayed a Sunday afternoon of many years earlier. I chased him behind one side of the brand-new, brown-and-orange sofa; we emerged on the opposite side. Grinning and giggling, we ran around our grandparents' living room again and again. As the film cycle clicked into darkness and the projector clicked off, the silence screamed.

His brother and I sat on the chilled floor of his dimly lit, abandoned room. We sifted through remnants of his possessions, searching for peace for our own souls. Quietly, we intruded into his belongings. His brother uncovered a tidy stack of Sports Illustrated magazines featuring the trials and triumphs of the Denver Broncos and the University of Nebraska Cornhuskers football teams. As he flipped the pages, he voiced, barely above a whisper, "Remember how we use to fight about football?"

Rummaging through his top desk drawer, I discovered a stack of photographs. Slowly, I turned toward the lamp and placed one behind the others to see each photograph. His strained family portrait taken three years earlier topped the stack, followed by my school pictures from the past four years and two of my dance team shots. A couple friends' school photos. And finally, a snapshot he captured in Seattle just as a lowering drawbridge was silhouetted by the dusking sun.

On top of his desk, his brother noticed a stack of perfectly clipped *Calvin and Hobbes* comic strips. Scanning them, he read them slowly to me. Quietly, we snickered together. *Calvin and Hobbes* framed his humor and his brilliance within its simplicity. Somehow, despite the heaving unknowns, we experienced a transfer of humor and brilliance. An unconscious weight ... we carry.

A couple decades before, two young brothers married two young sisters in a small country church planted on the prairie in Wyoming. A couple years later, he—Carlton Jamison Plinsky—was born to one couple. Seven weeks later, I was born to the other. Since our families lived so close, we grew up nearly inseparable. Grandma Ruth often chanted her revised version of the "Jack & Jill" nursery rhyme: "Jamie and Heidi went up a hill to fetch a pail of water. Jamie fell down and broke his crown. And Heidi came tumbling after." Jamie sat on her right knee while I sat on her left as she told us story after story with her ageless grin. "Jamie gets so tickled!" she'd say time and time again. I can still hear his laugh echo in the confines of my mind.

We shared family; we shared memories. We shared humor as well as questions as we grew older. Our extended family's structured strictness often stirred us to question. While we recognized the necessity of guidance, we often discussed our opinions of what we perceived as harsh rules. We wondered. We may have mocked. Mainly, we navigated our childhood together.

We no longer make memories, share humor or questions.

My dad quietly told me the news. Dropping to my knees, I sobbed hysterically. Time froze. Sleep evaded me. Shock overtook me. Thus, I wrestled to rein in every pelting thought until we arrived at his home pulsing with people, but lifeless without him.

The sheriff's report read, "On January 18, 1992, at approximately 7 p.m., seventeen-year-old Carlton Plinsky committed suicide while visiting the lodge with a youth group. Authorities say Plinsky hung himself with a cord taken from his duffel bag. He tied the cord to the ladder of the bunk bed. ..."

Just two months earlier, Thanksgiving of 1991, he and I spent hours watching football, sharing thoughts, and exchanging questions. Despite his gaze—distant and sad—his stance appeared more confident and his demeanor more peaceful. Our family, our holiday, and our lives sighed, "normal."

My parents and I took him to the airport. As he walked slowly down the terminal ramp, my dad yelled some crazy (maybe even bordering on coarse) joke. Jamie turned his head over his left shoulder and LAUGHED. I saw him laugh. I heard him laugh. But sometime between Thanksgiving and January 18, he stopped laughing.

Pens and Professors

Over 25 years ago, my pen began inking what my voice could not yet articulate. Four years into the grief of losing my cousin and dear friend, I wrote the preceding text as an in-class writing assignment for Advanced English Composition. "He Stopped Laughing" was written January 24, 1996. My English professor held me after class to say she thought with a few edits, the piece might be publishable. Little did she know how fragile I felt even penning the content. Despite the growing acknowledgement that Jamie's earthly life was over, her words encouraged me in my shifting life.

Another encouragement came from one of my counseling professors, who also suggested publication after a critical evaluation. He recommended I read *A Grief Observed* by C.S. Lewis, and I eagerly devoured Lewis' honest, immediate ailments of grief. His vulnerability stirred courage within me—I don't have to wait until I feel strong enough to start sharing. The strength of my writing may come through my weakness.

I lift up my eyes to the mountains—where does my help come from?
My help comes from the LORD, the Maker of heaven and earth.
Psalm 121:1-2

dark night

"Face to face with evil, Jesus was outraged; face to face with suffering and sin, Jesus wept. And if it were not for that anger and
those tears and the resolute road to the cross that they marked, we
could not realize how outraged God is by evil and how seriously
he takes sin."
Os Guinness
God in the Dark

That first night, after the initial news and cascading cries, hours
slipped away. I found myself both exhausted and wide awake. I
crawled into bed wanting and needing sleep but frightened of
dreaming. A dear friend, Alex, braved that night with me over the phone.
Neither of us remember much of the words exchanged in those many
hours. He was not sure Jamie actually died by what I said at first. I do

remember talking a lot as if to fill an unidentifiable void. I feared the dark and the inevitable silence to come. Alex's unflinching presence comforted even as shock faded. An unplanned response and a welcome grace.

Death silenced Jamie. Suddenly, I felt it, too—a silence I didn't understand. An absence. An intrusion. It felt both foreign and serene. Some silence quiets questions. Some silence calms chaos. Some silence honors the sacred. Some silence harbors fears, guilt, shame ... the unspeakable, a realm relegated away before death and darkness groaned too close.

And the dark encroached as the silence encamped.

During 1992, I knew it all felt heavy, cloudy, dark, and distant. But I didn't really find words until St. John of the Cross' work, "Dark Night of the Soul," expressed the mingling melee of invisible yet grounded truth sparring with anger, absence, and ongoing grief.

He writes, "Souls begin to enter this dark night when God proceeds to lead them from the state of beginners ... so that they may know the weakness of their state, and pluck up courage, and desire that God may set them in this night, wherein the soul is strengthened and confirmed in virtue and made ready for inestimable delights of the love of God."

Over the many years, I have been trained in the Scriptures, hymns, and even some church history. Somewhere along the way, I learned to look and linger in the Psalms as a songbook for our souls. The beauty. The patterns and the progression. A place to pause. To put words to my heart's cry when all alone. I also gleaned elements of church history as past pillars for future hope hunting, even in this present dark night.

First, Psalms 120-134 are known as the Psalms of Ascent. Some believe these psalms were part of the preparation and journey of the Hebrew people when they traveled to Jerusalem for the festivals a few times a year. They were a canticle carrying them through remembering, repenting, reconciling, and reminding one another of God's character even amidst their lamentable and lively circumstances. The psalms prepared them individually to purge and to receive a purification as they reunited to celebrate their creator and celebrate his light among them.

Years ago, Brennan Manning coined the phrase "doxology in the dark" in his book, *Ruthless Trust*. I'd been accustomed to praising God for his goodness and faithfulness in the world I could see. The sunrises and sunsets. The seedtime and the harvest. The rain and the roots. But here, all felt paused. How does an absence constrain and almost blind one in acute and present grief? Yes, I knew his nearness amidst. Yet an almost involuntary, temporary stiffening of soul wondered when this would all lift, so I could sing again.

Whispers of psalms and song rose mysteriously amidst this time. Melodies and words penned in generations past were passed down through simple gatherings and repeating together. This simple yet sturdy framework girded and guided, foreshadowing a future and tangible hope.

Immortal, invisible, God only wise,
In light inaccessible hid from our eyes,
Most blessed, most glorious, the Ancient of Days,
Almighty, victorious, Thy great name we praise.

Unresting, unhasting, and silent as light,
Nor wanting, nor wasting, Thou rulest in might;
Thy justice like mountains high soaring above
Thy clouds which are fountains of goodness and love.

To all life Thou givest, to both great and small;
In all life Thou livest, the true life of all;
We blossom and flourish as leaves on the tree,
And wither and perish, but nought changeth Thee.

> Great Father of Glory, pure Father of Light
> Thine angels adore Thee, all veiling their sight;
> All laud we would render, O help us to see:
> 'Tis only the splendor of light hideth Thee.
>
> Immortal, invisible, God only wise,
> In light inaccessible hid from our eyes,
> Most blessed, most glorious, the Ancient of Days,
> Almighty, victorious, Thy great name we praise.
>
> **Walter Chalmers Smith**
> "Immortal, Invisible, God Only Wise" (1857)

The palpable difference between being alive and yielding to eternal living often pulses the brightest evidence in our darkest grappling. "O help us to see." What grace and patience he offers as his nearness does not wane—even as our awareness might for a time.

> "Our design ... is only to discover how, perceiving a suffering world, and being assured, on quite different grounds, that God is good, we are to conceive that goodness and that suffering without contradiction."
> **C.S. Lewis**
> *The Problem of Pain*

After being privy to Jamie's slow suffocation with depression and his sinking under the shadow of death via suicide, I remember recognizing my own labored breath. The staccato, involuntary panting of shock slowly subsided. Each inhale and exhale, once instinct, now demanded mindful, labored efforts—efforts I feared I simply wasn't strong enough to muster and maintain.

No matter my confusion or ever-so-human desire to get through this, somehow this epic journey was unearthing and unfolding deeper, purer parts. What felt like an unresolved rush to speak whispered a heavenly hush and promise of unveiling to come.

For a time, my mind attempted to fight the coils of questions with self-sufficiency. Soon, my own spirit collapsed within me. I may have been alive; I wasn't the one our family buried in the ground. However, grief prodded my broken heart incessantly. Since Jamie and I were so close and everyone knew it, all eyes followed me.

However, I didn't know the steps to this dark dance, and my stage expressions couldn't conceal the seething weakness. The gravity of grief gives way to a raw reality too heavy for improv.

In the years since, I related to Jim Carrey's character in *The Truman Show*. While it would have been utterly ego-centric of me to assume the remaining attention (which prior to his death, I would have snagged eagerly) ought to fixate on me, I felt the stare of focus.

My mom worked in human resources at a large public school district. Her access to counselors and statistical data spotlighted me as a possible copycat. I don't know that she ever even verbalized this to me then, but as an intuitive only child, I sensed the concerned squints hovering around me.

For the first time in my life, all I wanted to do was escape and hide. Maybe in silent isolation, this paralyzing ache would evaporate and normal could return. Virtually all of me paused for quite some time. The outside of me continued to go through the motions of my existence while the inside conflicted between containment and collapse.

While I recognized the loving desire of family and friends to genuinely care, their grief and confusion heaved and hid, too. At the time, I could not have formulated words to describe it all.

I just knew I didn't want to add to the burdens already there.

I felt responsible for them. I felt responsible for Jamie. It was all more than I could bear, and I hated feeling this weak. If living was what was left for me, I didn't know how anymore.

High school fashions, gossip, and pressures shrunk away, as did a grander purpose for living. And dying demanded a response.

In this heavy haze, I heard the faint whispers of my own wandering prayers. Oh, how I wanted to keep Jamie alive—who he was, not just to me, but everyone fortunate to know him. His logic. His eloquence. His kindness. His quiet wit. People claim the deceased "live on in our hearts" or "as long as you have memories, he's still with you." Honestly, these feathery words felt empty to me.

When I was asked to be either a pallbearer or honorary pallbearer (one given a seat of honor, but no heavy lifting required), my acceptance of honorary over actual pallbearer brewed out of my hesitancy to accept the permanence of his death and to assist willingly in tucking his memory into decomposing soil. Neither could I passively accept his absence, nor could I actively endorse his choice.

Somehow I knew the weight of death in a box—no matter how strong I wanted to be—was too heavy for me.

His choosing suicide still perplexed me. C.S. Lewis suggests, "Suicide is the typical expression of the stoic spirit and the battle of the warrior spirit." Jamie, the bright and mostly compliant overachiever, recognized immediate gratifying paths led to meaninglessness. He willingly worked hard and focused. From building blocks to aviation, his devotion to the process and enjoyment in the successful steps along the way yielded visions far beyond his mere seventeen years. While the methodical details he marked in ending his own life fit him eerily, I didn't want to believe he really did it ... to himself. How could he?

During much of our childhood, I felt like I followed his lead. He set the academic bar of achievement high. Before we even started kindergarten, he was reading. I remember listening to him and watching him read words. Then sentences. And yes, paragraphs.

His abilities inspired me to sit still a little longer. This enabled me to give phonics time to saturate. Competition edged out my previous excuses to put off learning to read myself. Like Tom Cruise's character in *Top Gun*, I found flying in second place to Jamie easy, manageable. Freeing, really. He set the standard, and I dared to catch up to him as fast as I could.

But his demise left me soloing in the darkness, left me fumbling and fragile. I remember my role at the funeral included entering and exiting in an honored lineup. I vowed to be strong enough that day. I remember feeling like I trudged through, feeling the spotlight. "This must be the worst of it," I thought. With shallow breaths, I silenced my interior groans and screams—securely away, somewhere deep.

Strong enough to live without him? Strong enough to live out his potential and mine? Strong enough to see beyond the present shroud cloaking me? Cloaking all of us?

No, the worst was yet to come. We grew up primed by the prevalent worldview that perpetuates seizing obstacles by virtue of self-will alone. If I think it, I seize it. I win.

One problem for go-getter, hustle types? Since I'm still here, I thought I must live this thing called life brilliantly for the both of us. I even attempted to embody a few of his character qualities, the distinctly effortless part of him, so foreign to me.

Grief's grip was strangling me. And my fight? Weak, frantic, and hidden, as best as I could manage.

Paradoxically, I became nearly transfixed and self-focused on self-protection while I also sought to think of others well above myself. Before his departure, this would have been much more out of the ordinary; however, after he left ... well ...

When one loses a loved one to suicide, the rejection of kinship often severs a confidence in the survivor to extend friendship. Because my friendship resume includes loss to suicide, I wondered how many

ways I had failed him, and I feared failure might result in all relationships. I was just outgoing enough to easily hide in arenas of conversation and service. Instead of really connecting, I found socializing
actually helped me escape. Reminiscent of C.S. Lewis' thoughts, I
found means to live in a crowd. For a time, "caucus replaced friendship." All this while barely breathing beside people while the longing
for friendship deepened.

Strong enough. Strive enough. Serve enough.
... but I am not enough.

In this state of cloudy grief, I returned to a large public high school.
God chose to use my friend, Amy, in my sixth hour Algebra 2 class, to
breath his word into me. How? Amy slipped hand-written note cards
with Bible verses to me periodically through the remainder of our spring
semester. Imagine a high school junior thoughtfully taking the time to
scratch out a verse or two to pass to me discreetly during class. Simple.
Personal. And life-lifting.

At first, I couldn't even read them. Why not? Another well-mean-
ing friend approached me within the first 72 hours of Jamie's death
with this encouragement: "You know, Heidi, the Lord doesn't give us
anything we can't handle. He's prepared you for this." In my cloud of
confusion and grief, I thought to myself, "What if this God holds me
responsible for all I know of his word? What if he's testing my reliance
and resilience?"

Again ... not enough.

I remember making a decision—not against God himself, for I
still awed and revered him—but against acquiring more of his word
into my heart or mind out of pure exhaustion and fear of ongoing
testing. Several months would pass before I could pick up my own
leather-bound Bible.

"The darker the night, the brighter the stars. The deeper the grief, the closer is God."
Fyodor Dostoyevsky
Crime and Punishment

This season of darkness illuminated vague and heavy fears I'd not known before and could not yet name. Eventually, I recognized failure. I feared I failed Jamie. I feared I failed the family.

However, Holy Scriptures found me in a quiet corner of a public high school. I found sanctuary as his love poured out in his word, hand-delivered on 3x5 cards by my friend who knew only one balm for my heart's puncture wound. I'm not sure I've ever thanked her enough. Her simple obedience to keep reaching out quietly rooted my once-rocky faith in Jesus.

Through his living word, handwritten heart to heart, "the things of this world will grow strangely dim in the light of his glory and grace," as the great hymn puts it. God is referenced as the lifter of heads in the Psalms. He tenderly reached out to me. Personally. Patiently. Lifting my gaze. He tenderly revealed his presence pulsing within his people ... within me.

The weight of death was no longer a far-off illusion or distant imaginary event. Though the grim reaper was not visible, his heated breath and swiping claws barreled about me. I remember reading David's description in 2 Samuel 22:5-7. I felt anguish and understanding. I felt horrified and heard. I felt isolated yet not alone.

The waves of death swirled about me; the torrents of destruction
overwhelmed me. The cords of the grave coiled around me;
the snares of death confronted me. In my distress I called to the
LORD; I called out to my God. From his temple
he heard my voice; my cry came to his ears.
2 Samuel 22:5-7

"Discovering myself loved by God and forging new dimensions
of intimacy with God's presence had brought healing to my fragmented life."
C.S. Lewis
The Problem of Pain

Entering every day recognizing, "He's really gone." "He's not coming
back." No matter what vivid dreams of him in crowded halls or traf-
fic-jammed parking lots, I awoke... still alone...wondering, "Do I have
what it takes to make it through?"

We blossom and flourish as leaves on the tree,
And wither and perish, but nought changeth Thee.

James 1 became my heartbeat.

Consider it pure joy, my brothers, when you face trials of many
kinds because you know the testing of your faith produces
perseverance. Perseverance must finish its work, so that
you may be mature and complete, not lacking anything. If any
of you lacks wisdom, he should ask God, who gives generously
to all without finding fault, and it will be given to him.
James 1:2-5

Blessed is the man who remains steadfast under trial,
for when he has stood the test he will receive the crown of life,
which God has promised to those who love him.
James 1:12 (ESV)

Let us hold unswervingly to the hope we profess, for
he who promised is faithful. And let us consider how we
may spur one another on toward love and good deeds.
Hebrews 10:23-24

I don't have what it takes to carry on ... but I know Who does.

And then, after the snow-shrouded funeral, as grief languishes but schedules resume and demands demand again, tired, weary ... we recognized this heavy defining time. Is life livable without him?

The void and its clamoring questions clouded my every thought. Every waking moment required my involvement. Where is the clarity? The purpose? Every action, once routine, sucked what little energy my mind agreed lendable to my body.

We blossom and flourish as leaves on the tree,
And wither and perish, but nought changeth Thee

I remember somewhere along my academic journey learning many plants grow at night. Particularly, the roots grow deep in the predawn hours when dew eases movement among the soil. So, too, for me during this time. I felt I lost my childhood, but I also felt a sense of growing compassion and unfettered hope at the same time.

Scouring libraries, my seventeen-year-old self, who knew little outside studies, sports, and dancing, searched for confident voices pointing to real, tangible brave beauty in suicide's wake. While surrounded by what was busy and ordinary, fear and sadness nearly convinced me I was treading these icy waters utterly alone.

My research surfaced two primary focuses for the subject of suicide. First, the list of "warning signs" and urgent instruction to seek help. And second, if one is facing a loss including suicide, another list of "grieving steps" to anticipate or plan to go through. Not at all what I hoped to find.

I wanted to hear other people articulate how suicide didn't steal their breath and enslave them to a joyless existence, not clinical books with clinical examples. Skeptically, I wanted to quiet the questions and find courage to live—without forgetting.

There, the Lord picked me up and put me on a pilgrimage of prayer. In those early days, I think I was looking more for comfort, empathy, and creative understanding—key qualities God possessed beyond this present darkness, and qualities I wanted. In *The Lily of the Field and The Bird of the Air*, Soren Kierkegaard wrote, "to pray is not to listen to oneself speak, but to come to keep silent, and to continue keeping silent, to wait, until the person who prays hears God."

This journey led me back to our family.

Our help is in the name of the LORD,
the Maker of heaven and earth.
Psalm 124:8

"Neither do people light a lamp and put it under a bowl. Instead
they put it on its stand, and it gives light to everyone in the house.
In the same way, let your light shine before others, that they may
see your good deeds and glorify your Father in heaven."
Matthew 5:15-16

lamp lighting

In the nearly suffocating darkness of Jamie's death, Hope extended salt, light, and songs again. The darkness bears down. Like a weight too heavy to lift. Slowly squeezing out every last breath. Yet it is here I met Hope anew. I learned to enter and experience grief and mourning and life again.

I searched bookstores and libraries for other families who traversed this dark path and found the light again, for I knew the light was, and is, there. As I walked those halls, I kept thinking: Maybe I need to reach out to my family.

Job 8:8-9 says, "Ask the former generations and find out what their fathers learned, for we were born only yesterday, and know nothing, and our days on earth are but a shadow."

So I asked them. Four generations. And several vulnerably shared distinctly personal elements of grief, sadness, and persistent struggle through this heavy darkness.

Each generation recognized the varying social stigmas of suicide as well as the responses of their closest friends. I am supremely grateful for their honesty. While we share common relationships, every memory is profoundly unique to those who cycle through them; yet our family's openness to sharing weaved threads of bravery within me. While they spoke, I penned their words ... and processed my own.

They shared this vulnerable gift with me, and they granted permission to share with you. Lamp-lighting perspectives. First lived, then voiced. Those voices may just be a song, calling us close. Quivering, flickering. Remembering. A mourning. Radiating. And a morning.

From our family to yours, though this remains tender for us, we welcome you.

We pray these voices cultivate deeper roots of hope, faith and fruitful compassion—even in the wrestling.

> "Each family on earth is a magic kingdom, and the spells that it casts are long-lasting and powerful."
> **Frederick Buechner**
> *The Eyes of the Heart: A Memoir of the Lost and Found*

The lamp-lighting perspectives in the pages that follow begin with a brief history of the family member written in the third person, a quick reflection of my oral interview with them, and then their first-person perspectives, transcribed by me and edited for length and clarity.

With that, allow me to introduce you to my family, listed below by their relationship to Jamie.

- Maternal great-grandparents Philip and Ruth
- Paternal great-grandmother Hazel
- Paternal grandfather Darrell

- Paternal grandmother Wanda
- Maternal grandfather Ken
- Maternal grandmother Phyllis
- Father Carlton
- Mother Kathy
- Brother Michael
- Sister Holly
- Aunt Karen (Kathy's sister)
- Uncle Tim (Carlton's brother)

As for me, I am Jamie's cousin, the only child of Tim and Karen.

Great-Grandparents Grieve

Philip and Ruth, Maternal Great-Grandparents

Brief Personal History

Philip's parents emigrated from Sicily prior to his birth in the early 1900s. He was the first American born of his immediate family. His mother spoke only Italian. He described his family as typical of Italian immigrants living in the Chicago area at the time. (Due to mob complications, he eventually changed his last name ... which is another story.)

When he married Ruth, he thought she was eighteen years old. She and her mother stretched the truth. She was fifteen. When the family teased her about this, her characteristic response: "Oh phooey, I was practically sixteen."

Ruth, the youngest of a Scotch-Irish family, loved people with blend of toughness and tenderness. Standing tall at five feet, she nuzzled in with tight hugs, squint-eyed smiles, and commonly pinched waists to determine how well we were eating. She never lost her youthful sense of adventure or her uncanny ability to speak the tough truths with deepest love—whether to family or those she was meeting for the first time.

Although cultural Catholicism was their extended family heritage, Philip and Ruth accepted Jesus as personal Savior and became practicing Protestants after they already had three children of their own.

Eventually, Philip graduated from Moody Bible Institute. He pastored congregations in the Great Plains, including Colorado, Nebraska, and Wyoming. His favorite hobby: fishing. Ruth fried those fish to everyone's delight, actively serving the communities they called home. In one of the Swedish settlements in southeast Wyoming, their only daughter, Phyllis, found her groom, Kenneth, a World War II hometown hero.

During retirement, Philip and Ruth spent several years wintering in south Texas or Florida and summering on their son-in-law and daughter's farm. When age slowed their bodies some, they relocated year-round to an assisted living facility, where they remained active socially. Ruth commonly checked in on those who entertained few visitors, read many books, and kept an immaculately tidy tiny home. Philip continued to watch boxing, write sermons, and find a good theological discussion with whomever he could engage.

Born June 27, 1905, Philip died January 26, 1999. Ruth was born September 10, 1910, and died April 6, 2003.

Reflections on the Interview

In July 1997, I interviewed our great-grandparents, Philip and Ruth LaBue. Between the emotional weight of the conversation and issues with hearing loss, I opted to interview them together. Even five years after Jamie died, they needed each other to even speak about him and especially the manner of his death. I wish you could have heard the rising voices as well as the faint whispers. I wish you could have seen her tenderly patting his arm as he wiped the endless flow of tears. When one slowed thoughts and speech, the other spoke up, repeating in agreement or adding to clarify.

Beyond the slow gate and sun-sagging skin radiated an enduring love. They learned, lived, and laughed a rhythm together for over seven decades, adoring each other immensely. And they spilled that adoration over our entire family. Our earliest lessons of discipline and love came from them.

As you read their perspective, there are two things to note. First, I compiled notes from the transcripts to write their perspective in a collective voice rather than conduct separate interviews resulting in individual voices. Unless otherwise noted with "I (individual name)," their "we" voice reflects both of them.

Additionally, I intentionally did not edit or downplay their theological conversation points. Many question the theological implications of suicide. Some prefer to avoid such questions altogether. These questions are not my primary focus. My primary focus remains our discovery of living hope beyond the shadow of death. In a pluralistic day like ours, the inclusion of such wrestling as well as subsequent findings may stir additional discomfort and potential disagreement among readers. Their words are shared as an honest reflection of their hearts' life beat.

Lamp-lighting Perspective

Before delving into this most difficult subject in our long lives, we must convey what has been most important in our lives. The Lord Jesus Christ touched us when we were young parents, and his touch changed us. Next only to him, our family is of supreme importance to us. Our definition of family includes blood relatives, their spouses, and every branch leading to us and flowing from us. We feel responsible for them no matter how old we are. We love to be with our family as often as we can; they are the joy of our lives.

We lived a great many years with many trials and pains within the family. Sadly, we endured loss in various forms: severed relationships, divorce, and death. How these struggles have pained us! When some of our grandchildren chose to divorce, we hurt so badly. Oh, how we wished we could do something to patch up the brokenness in those marriages!"

However, nothing could have prepared us for the pain of losing Jamie...

We remember the day Jamie was born. Instantly, we burst with pride! Summering in the north, we stayed on the same farm where our daughter and son-in-law (Phyllis and Ken) along with Jamie and his parents lived in three different homes on the homestead property.

Simply put, we had experienced nothing like the joys of retirement with strong bodies and minds. This great-grandson was like no other. We were blessed with other children before Jamie, but they lived more than a day's drive away. We experienced great-grandparenting differently because he lived close to us. We really got to enjoy him because we could focus on him—from sunup to sundown sometimes. We did not know the limitless love the Lord would provide us for other great-grandchildren until Heidi came along, and she stole our hearts as well.

From our front porch on the farm, Ken and Phyllis's home stood large to the right as Kenny had built on several times over the years to accommodate for the growing family, including a 24' x 24' living room. Oh, how we loved gathering there! While our summer home nestled behind the big house, Carlton and Kathy lived in the smaller house to our left. The summer of 1974, just before Jamie and Heidi were born, Kenny laid a concrete sidewalk connecting all three homes.

Anytime Kathy needed a break, she would send Jamie to our place. We had no idea how nice that sidewalk was going to be for those kids. And for us, too. With all that foot traffic, it sure helped keep the floors and entries cleaner. I can still see Jamie toddling along the sidewalk. We loved having those kids come over because they knew how to "mind" (Grandma Ruth translation for "obey").

Idleness is one of the seven deadly sins. We did our best to keep our kids busy. We attracted them with ice cream, rice pudding, and peanut butter by the spoonfuls. We required them to complete jobs before we enjoyed sitting down with them to watch television.

Jamie and Heidi—if she were over, too, as she lived on a different homestead—were often required to pick up sticks and took turns sweeping the porch. They were about three or four years old, but they knew what was required, how to do a good job (no "monkey business," another Grandma Ruth-ism), and they still loved being with us. And we loved having them. They would sit quiet and still for some time just watching

Grandpa bead fishing lures in his study. They would just sit there. Then, we would often watch *Hogan's Heroes* and *The Flintstones* together.

We took our pontoon out on the lake; those kids loved to go with us. Jamie's first night away from his parents was with us in our camper. Most of our memories from these years center around Jamie and Heidi. We used to sing the "Jack and Jill" nursery rhyme using "Jamie and Heidi" instead. They giggled. Then they looked at each other and laugh and laugh. Oh, they were just something else ... so cute.

One of my (Grandpa Philip) other hobbies was filming the family. Oh what fun I had filming the grandchildren! Moving pictures. Can you even imagine such a thing? Well, in your day and age, I suppose you can. But this technology was new for us and fascinating for me. So I naturally continued to film the new batch of kids in the family. We could not get over how cute those two were together. Jamie, the smiley and happy one, endured Heidi scooting closer and closer to him trying to invade his space and tell him what to do or not to do. Those two were twins to us. Other people told us that often as well.

Jamie's parents remained on the farm for one year after their second child, Michael, was born (Jamie was about five years old at the time). That Michael. He was something else, too. Oh, how we loved every moment with those kids! And nothing was the same after they moved off the farm. We felt sick over it. We didn't get enough time with Michael. And with Jamie, well, we felt he was our own. We mourned the loss. We did not feel right about them moving. We argued and agonized over our own emotions because we felt like those kids were ours, too.

We only saw them once a year for short visits after that. Oh, how they changed from visit to visit. Jamie's mom communicated with us as to the kids' academic achievements and extracurricular activities. She sent photos from time to time. We knew Jamie worked hard and did very well in school. As years passed, he seemed to become shyer and less smiley. He struggled with allergies and horrible sores in his mouth.

They said the sores were stress related. Why was a young boy stressed? We didn't know.

The last time Jamie was in our home he had traveled with Heidi and her parents to celebrate Thanksgiving at Ken and Phyllis's. We invited Jamie and Heidi, now teenagers, to stay with us in our apartment at the assisted living facility. They accepted our invitation. As always, we were so glad they wanted to see us.

Jamie seemed to struggle going to sleep. He mentioned he was suffering from headaches as well. Each night they stayed with us, we had to say, "Now Jamie, you need to put that light out and get some sleep." He did not quarrel; simply and quickly, he obeyed. He seemed restless much of the visit.

Yet, we saw him happy on that visit as well. I (Grandma Ruth) slipped him $5 to take Heidi to Wendy's for a light lunch. He accepted with a familiar smile. He and Heidi returned acting silly. It was so nice to see an older version of what we remembered of them: carefree kids still finishing each other's sentences. When they were about two, they would chase each other like puppies. One chasing the other around one side of the sofa only to be chased around the other side. We laughed and laughed.

I (Grandma Ruth) remember speaking to him, "Say, Jamie, you are growing into a handsome young man!" And he replied with a smirk, "I know, Grandma!"

I (Grandpa Philip) remember feeling sorry for him because something seemed to be haunting him. One evening, he was switching the off and on button on the remote control for the television repetitively. I rebuked him. He did not quarrel. I still feel bad because I did not take the time to ask him what was bothering him. Instead, I rebuked him like that. Oh, how I wish I would have taken the time to ask. I think he would have told me ... if only I had asked.

Early in the morning on Sunday, January 19, 1992, our even-tempered Swedish son-in-law, Kenny, came over—which was unusual at that time because we were still driving ourselves to church then. He came in quieter than he normally did, his jaw clenched tight. But he spoke sternly and said, "Dad, better sit down."

The Italian in me went berserk. We have no words adequate to articulate how we felt. He could have put a bullet in *my* head. I (Grandpa Philip) went crazy! I just kept shouting, "It can't be! Jamie committed suicide! Suicide! It can't be! Not Jamie! Not our Jamie! No! No! No!"

As vivid as those initial moments were, the many days following remain a distinct and literal blur due to the constant flow of tears. My eyes ached from the tearful drain. As with Job, "My face is foul with weeping, and on my eyelids is the shadow of death" (Job 16:16 KJV).

We knew we could not go to the funeral. We could not see Jamie lying in that box. We could not bear to face his parents ... not yet. We knew seeing their sorrow combined with our own would ignite a ghastly scene of uncontrollable emotion. Such a demonstrative demonstration would have been a disgrace. My (Grandpa Philip) grief, my remorse, my sorrow are feelings too strong for me.

As a child, I attended many Italian immigrant funerals. The emotional demonstrations included weeping, sobbing, and yelling. The rest of Jamie's family is not as demonstrative as I am, so I just knew I could not disgrace them.

Our grief, the week of the funeral, we bore alone. That was the way we felt best to honor the family.

During the days following, we kept repeating, "His poor mother! His poor mother! Oh, his dad! What are they going to do?"

Jamie's death took part of our life away. Nothing compares to his loss. Death is one thing, but suicide... Oh Jamie, didn't you know how much we loved you?

We did not think anything like this could happen in our family. We love our family too much. They love each other too much. We still don't understand. For a while, we did not want to see or talk to anyone. Grieving takes time. Jamie's mother sent us a copy of the funeral video; I

(Grandpa Philip) just cannot watch it. I still can't bear it. After Grandma watched it, she looked straight at me, pointed her finger, and said, "If anything happens to Heidi, don't tell me!"

Suicide. How repulsive! Before Jamie's death, we thought someone who kills himself must be a coward or sick in the mind. Only a troubled person in need of attention with problems that needed to be solved—seeing no other way out or seeking escape—could even consider such an act. And now, we feel so sorry for a person (and his family) who ends his life because he cannot seem to find strength to live it. Oh, those left behind. How deep the grief! Knowing we all ask the answerless questions, we wonder in hindsight, "What could we have done to help?"

We think of Job from Scripture. Oh, how he suffered! Losing his family, property, and health, he cried out, "Naked I came from my mother's womb, naked I shall return. The Lord gives; the Lord takes away. Blessed be his name." Yet, we continue to battle disappointment with God. Not anger. We know God does not make mistakes, but we struggle with the almost hopeless finality of suicide. In dark sorrow, we forget the sovereignty of God for moments; we don't want to do that. So, we keep the Scriptures close. I (Grandpa Philip), though retired, still write sermons, which keeps me thinking and praying and healing, I hope.

A natural death seems easier to accept as God's timing. We lost one of our sons to an accident a few years before Jamie. While inspecting a roof of a commercial building, our son fell through a skylight and never regained consciousness. Oh, the pain we felt at his loss! However, he enjoyed full life with wonderful children and grandchildren. His loss was easier to accept than Jamie's.

Knowledge and reviewing Scripture comforts us with peace, faithful assurance, and hope for eternal rest in heaven. This is denied to those who blaspheme the Holy Spirit and reject Jesus. All other sins are forgivable. Jamie broke one of the commandments by taking his own life, but he also confessed Jesus as Lord.

Romans 10:9-10 says, "That if you confess with your mouth, Jesus is Lord, and believe in your heart that God raised him from the dead, you will be saved. For it is with your heart that you believe and are justified and it is with your mouth that you confess and are saved."

We believe the Lord when he says, "He who comes to me I will not cast out" (John 6:37).

Jamie's life reflected that of a faithful servant. Even as a teenager, he volunteered in the church with children and the sound equipment. He was gentle, kind, and thoughtful of others. We could see his heart by the way he lived his life.

Yet, his mind was troubled. We speculate his choice to go on a retreat at Christian camp was an effort to settle some of his thinking. The torment must have been so heavy. We know we don't understand what he faced. As time has passed, picturing Jamie at peace—walking the streets of gold, free from that torment—does give us some comfort. We believe we will join him in a joyous reunion one day.

In time, we go from seeing, hearing, smelling, tasting, and feeling our pain and misunderstandings to seeing how this kind of pain and loss can serve goodness as well. First, we are drawn to seek God even more in our confusion and hurt. We think harder about how we interact with others, and we are reminded to value and communicate that value to those we treasure.

I (Grandma Ruth) speak of Jamie often. Oh, how we miss that boy! Grandpa can only handle so much talk of Jamie, so I share with several people in our assisted living building. They are touched. Then they ask questions which lead into sharing Jesus in such a personal way. As Romans 8:28 says, "God is working all these things together for the good to those who are called according to His purpose."

Pain and sorrow continue, but seeing the good restores our joy at the same time. Mysterious metamorphosis occurs during grieving. Our heart aches so much for our only remaining twin, Heidi. Her sorrow must be so severe because they were so close from birth. We wish we could take that pain away, but we just can't.

We try not to dwell on the manner of his death anymore as it conjures up so many unanswerable questions: What could we have done differently? Why was his pain so deep? Why didn't anyone see how much he was hurting?

These thoughts seem to reopen the deep grief wound. I (Grandpa Philip) cry every time we speak of his death. I hate suicide! Not the person who dies, but the grief he leaves behind! I hate it! Some have said all this would get easier. As the years go by for us, the reality of Jamie's absence is still so difficult.

When Heidi got married, we thought Jamie should be standing up with Alex. Imagine what a marvelous man—husband, dad, pilot, doctor—he could have become. He had no idea his place in our family, in history, or his potential to better the world.

Oh, how we miss him! If we live to be 100 years old, we will never understand it! We just can't. Simply, we choose to remember Jamie's life and the joy he brought to our family. We share our perspectives because we still love Jamie and miss him terribly. And we know we're not the first family to face this or the last, so we speak love and life into the silent places where the shadow of death has convinced the grieving they must sink in their deep sadness and remain silent because suicide is a shameful stain on a family. We believe it is a wrong choice with unimaginable painful consequences, but we also believe God is greater than our pain. He is good. His grace is sufficient.

"Naked I came from my mother's womb, and naked
hall I return. The Lord gave, and the Lord has taken away;
blessed be the name of the Lord."
Job 1:21 (ESV)

Great-Grandmother's Endurance

Hazel, Paternal Great-Grandmother

Brief Personal History

Hazel Fern Schafer Plinsky Neel was born March 10, 1906. She grew up and lived her life in rural Kansas. Hardworking. Content. Kind. Practical. Classy.

She endured much in her life, including the loss of two husbands. She penned some of her own life memories in May 2001, describing the pipeline being built when she was a school girl and the response from her small town. She wrote of improving race relations through children playing together and community potlucks. She acknowledged being a bit hungry during the Dust Bowl years. The depravation of the Great Depression? She wrote that she really did not notice too much until a government official stopped in to inquire about the living conditions and how she and her husband, Ernie, were feeding the farming family. From her notes:

> One day before the pipeline came through a lady came to the door. I was ironing and heating flat irons on the cook stove. She started asking questions, so I began to ask who she was and why all these personal questions ... about our food, clothing, and income, etc.
>
> For instance, she asked, "What did you have for breakfast?" I said toast, coffee, and Ernie had two eggs. The boys, Darrell and Dean, each had one egg and a

glass of milk. (We didn't have Carolyn yet.) Then, she asked again what I ate. I said, "Toast and coffee." She wanted to know why I didn't have an egg. I told her that we only had a few hens and without proper feed, they didn't lay many eggs.

She looked at me and said, "Lady, you are on a starvation diet." She almost made me feel sorry for myself. She kept asking other questions about our other meals. When she asked where Ernie ate lunch, I said I sent lunch with him. I made a sandwich with mustard on one slice and butter on the other one—no fruit. She almost fell from her chair and told me that in a few days someone would be bringing us some food.

I was so curious about so many things and asked so many questions. She finally said she wasn't supposed to tell us, but it was a government deal and was free as long as we needed it. Of course, I looked for it every day, but Uncle Sam is never in a big hurry to do things for us (only when he wants our taxes). But in due time, someone did come with lots of food: flour, rice, canned meat, canned peaches, and corn meal that I remember.

We never met our great-grandfather, Ernie. Our dads never met him either, as he passed away just a month after my dad was born and well before Jamie's dad was born. Great-grandma Hazel, on the other hand, lived to be 98. She died on February 19, 2005.

Reflections on the Interview

Great-grandma Hazel not only agreed to participate in my project to collect the family memories and ponderings, but she quietly endorsed my efforts to encourage other families who face similar loss.

Initially, I sent a questionnaire to each family member to fill out before our recorded interview. Grandma Hazel filled in the sheets with brevity and reverence.

She died before I had the opportunity to seek more understanding from her. However, I think her brief, guarded responses illustrate perfectly the varying distinctions grief maneuvers among us. Some personalities (and maybe even some seasons) need to put words to all they deal with in order to move forward while others move forward more privately ... without such words.

Grief is not a state to ignore, hide or mask, but a path leading to perseverance and perspective. For a dear lady who endured hardship and embodied joy with such grace and dignity, I am deeply grateful for her life example as well as her selective use of words.

Lamp-lighting Perspective

Oh, Jamie. He was a loving and caring young man. Polite. Smart. A very young man.

Due to my age and limited travel as well as his family's move to Denver, I seldom got to see Jamie and the family. I stayed in my small town mostly. And the younger ones moved around more. Times change. I understood that. But I so enjoyed preparing gifts for my whole family every January for Christmas several months later.

On the night of January 18, 1992, I was wrapping Christmas gifts and very happy until word came about what happened.

Very sad ... such a young man.

The last time I remember seeing Jamie was my 85th birthday party. I saw him walk up the stairs and thought how nice looking and sweet a person he is ... that is how I remember Jamie.

Very, very sad ... wondering why.

"Honest writing shows us how badly we are living and how good life is. Enlightenment is not without pain. But the pain, accepted and endured, is not a maiming, but a purging."

Eugene Peterson
Run With the Horses

Remembering Mercy

Darrell, Paternal Grandfather

Brief Personal History

Grandpa Darrell was born July 16, 1924, the firstborn child to Ernie and Hazel Plinsky. His family farmed. He attended a one-room schoolhouse from grade school through high school in Beverly, Kansas. An athlete, he lettered in basketball, football, and baseball and was known for throwing a mean knuckleball.

He attended Bethany College in Lindsborg, Kansas, prior to farming some for his Uncle Herman. Darrell served in the US Navy during the war. After boot camp, he was sent to the Aleutian Islands, Alaska, where he boarded the ATR-32, a fire fighting vessel traveling with a fleet of ships bound to bombard the Japanese islands.

At the end of World War II, Darrell returned to his hometown. He received many letters from Wanda during his many months away. He made a point to see her the first night home. About a year later, they were married. They raised three sons (David, Timothy, and Carlton—Jamie's dad) and two daughters (Lori and Gretchen). Darrell also attended Bible college in Colorado. He spent his working years at Quartzite Stone Co. (two years) and Tweco Manufacturing Co. (thirty-seven years). Additionally, he was an active member of Calvary Bible Church for fifty years, serving in roles such as Sunday School teacher and deacon.

My dad, Tim, has memories of Grandpa Darrell's morning routine. He was a runner before running was cool, and he would get up before the rest of the family stirred, starting every day reading the Bible and on his knees in prayer. This quiet consistency laid a solid foundation for my dad, who did the same for me.

At this writing, Grandpa Darrell is in his nineties, still living independently and maintaining home projects, although his pace has slowed some. He and Grandma Wanda continue to faithfully pray for their entire family every day, plus any additional heartfelt concerns for any within their circle. I'm deeply grateful for their persevering love and care for each of us, far and near. They are a true testimony of consistency and joy to our family.

Reflections on the Interview

On January 13, 2007, I interviewed Grandpa Darrell and Grandma Wanda individually at the Wichita, Kansas, home where they raised their family. Before the interview, both wrote multiple pages in their own handwriting along with filling out the initial project survey I sent them. This made the interview much easier for me, as I could ask them to expound some or recount what they had already penned.

As I was preparing to go on a writing retreat following these interviews, I decided last minute to ask Grandpa to describe himself. I love his succinct reply. (Can you tell Grandma Hazel was his Mom?)

"Think before I speak. (Hoping what I say is right.) Much less talkative than my wife."

(That last line he punctuated with a smile.)

Grandpa's ease and peace stood out to me throughout our conversation. While thoughtful when choosing his words, he confidently spoke in his soft-spoken manner. Although this conversation was nearly 15 years after Jamie's death, Grandpa Darrell did not seem to camp too long on the questions. His desire: Remember Jamie. Be grateful daily to the Lord for his grace, mercy, and constant comfort.

Lamp-lighting Perspective

That Saturday evening in January of 1992 found us at our older daughter's home caring for their children as she and her husband went out for the evening. Wanda answered the phone. She broke down as she handed the phone to me. I knew something serious had happened, a critical injury or a death. Although naturally talkative, Wanda is not one to emotionally react like that without sufficient cause. The caller? Our youngest son, Jamie's dad.

He methodically explained all he knew up to that point in time. I listened. What do you do when your youngest son calls to report his first-born child is gone—gone ... at his own hand? What do you do? Listen. Before we hung up the phone, we prayed.

That next morning, our flight arranged easily as our son worked for a major airline. We were grateful for that. The airlines made the flights, and the employees made it comfortable. We made our way to Denver. In shock, I remember meeting family there. Few details remain. Such a time of intense sadness.

Several days were spent together with family and relatives awaiting Jamie's body released from the morgue in the mountains and transported to Denver. Wanda and I went with Carlton and Kathy to the funeral home to choose a casket and vault. Over the years, Wanda and I had buried both our dads along with a stepfather. In addition, recent to that time, we made all the funeral arrangements for Wanda's mother, so we had some idea our limited experience would be helpful at such a time. We appreciated the funeral home representative who was respectful, helpful, and non-pressuring. He left us alone so we could take the time we needed to think through all the details. We are simple people, so deciding how many pillows are sufficient for burial can seem complicated. Difficult though it was, Wanda and I were thankful we could be of some help in this process.

Then the day came. All the men of the family went to the funeral home to view the body before the rest. Tears flooded me. My expression: "What a waste!" A whole, hopeful life ahead. Jamie was so intelligent and hard-working, humble and compassionate. He could have been a doctor, a lawyer, or a businessman, but he did not grant himself the opportunity to live out his capabilities. Those seventeen years were not a waste, but all I could see, as a grandfather at that moment, was all he had ahead of him. Vanished.

> "I stood beside the coffin a few moments, my brain a turmoil of confusion. Grief, loss, and pity flooded over me, but the most overwhelming feeling was one of waste. For those who are desperately ill, death can be a welcome relief. Sudden deaths by accident or heart failure always shock and devastate. But suicide, deliberate self-destruction, especially of a talented and gifted young person, appalls. The unfulfilled dreams, the unfinished work, the uncompleted promise mock like demons."
>
> **G. Lloyd Carr and Gwendolyn C. Carr**
> *The Fierce Goodbye: Hope in the Wake of Suicide*

After those intense moments, God's grace did a healing work, helping me to focus more on being thankful for the remaining family members, especially the grandchildren. God granted strength to free my focus from this horrible death and shift it to the life we who remain are called to live.

About two weeks later, Wanda and I traveled back to Carlton and Kathy's to help them go through Jamie's books, clothes, and other possessions, a difficult endeavor after any death. I remembered my own father's death. He passed on when I was a young father with only two of our five children born at the time. My mother told me then, "As hard as it may be, we must get rid of all the clothes and other personal possessions of the dead loved one as quickly as possible to prevent lingering sorrow." Although I did not want to forget Jamie, I shared this wisdom from my mother with Carlton and Kathy because they needed to shift their focus from his death to the lives they still had with Michael and Holly as well as with one another.

Death changes people, and I am not referring to the one who dies. I observed firsthand the damage that can happen at the time of death back in World War II. While operating a US Army tank, my cousin Gerald was killed in Tunisia, Africa, by a German shell. His death caused his parents great sorrow, especially for his dad, my Uncle Herman.

Uncle Herman's persistent focus on his son's death rather than his life contributed to a lengthy time of bitterness. He harbored much anger toward the Army, as well as the war in general. Later, Uncle Herman made difficult demands on his other, much younger son, as though he needed to fill in for his dead brother. I remember hearing remarks like, "You will never be able to do this work as good as your brother." This younger brother spent his life trying to do the impossible, even going to the extent of marrying a young lady he knew his father liked, only to divorce her as soon as his folks died.

This is the result of allowing sorrow to linger too long. The Bible makes reference to this as "eating ashes" or "feeding on aches." We have time to focus on the death leading up to the funeral, but then we must choose to live the life God has given to us.

My own dealing with the finality regarding Jamie's death came as I pondered the whole situation in my early-morning prayers. The thought came to me vividly: "Jamie is dead. He is gone. No way to bring him back ... life must go on."

> *"Come to me, all you who are weary and burdened,*
> *and I will give you rest. Take my yoke upon you and*
> *learn from me, for I am gentle and humble in heart,*
> *and you will find rest for your souls."*
> **Matthew 11:28-29**

He really was a thoughtful and kind young man. I do wish we could have seen him make it to adulthood and live up to his potential. I remember the good times and the pleasant things with Jamie. However, I will not linger my thinking and overly dwell on the sorrow.

"Cast all your anxiety on him because he cares for you."
1 Peter 5:7

Ultimately, I have been comforted by remembering Jamie's life and looking to the Lord for his daily guidance.

"Only as we remember and remind ourselves of God's faithfulness can we ever see the pattern God has woven in our lives and learn confidence in his working."
Ravi Zacharias
Cries of the Heart

In the years since, I have spoken to Wanda and our daughters Gretchen and Lori the most about Jamie. We still remember him with a smile.

My favorite memory of Jamie happened when we were vacationing with Carlton's family in Hawaii. As we stood on a high lookout point, the wind came sweeping across the hill. We all tensed to the brisk air. However, Jamie quietly approached me. With his jacket in hand, he lifted and—silently—offered it to me.

Beyond Brilliance

Wanda, Paternal Grandmother

Brief Personal History

Grandma Wanda was born February 28, 1930, on a farm in rural Kansas—just months after the stock market crash ushered in the Great Depression. Wanda Mae McGeary was the daughter of James Eber McGeary and Olive Anne Turner McGeary. She had two brothers and two sisters.

She started dating Grandpa Darrell when she was a junior in high school, the day he returned home from serving with the United States Navy during World War II.

In June of 1946, Grandma Wanda, nearly a senior in high school, paid a visit to a local pastor's wife. During their time together, Grandma invited Christ into her life. Although she wasn't personally raised in church, she did attend with Darrell during their dating season and off and on throughout her growing up years.

She graduated high school on May 20, 1947. She married Grandpa Darrell on June 29, 1947, adding Plinsky to her name. Together, they moved to Denver, Colorado, where Grandpa had enrolled in Denver Bible College (renamed Rockmont by the time he graduated).

Five children arrived, all born in different places: David (1948) in Denver; Timothy (1951, Heidi's dad) in Salina, Kansas; Carlton (1953, Jamie, Michael, and Holly's dad) in Harper, Kansas; Lori (1959) in Attica, Kansas; and Gretchen (1966) in Wichita. Home changed often until they moved to Wichita, but she remained a busy mother at each stop. In 1973, she began working at Christian Challenge School, where she remained full time until 1990. She continued to work the following decade doing food demonstrations until she fully retired in 2000.

Throughout her life, Grandma has been active in her church as well as hosting countless friends in her home. From game nights to widows' luncheons to celebrating her favorite time of year (Christmas), she is gifted with flavorful food and welcoming hospitality. Fried chicken? No one makes it like Grandma. And her colorfully tasty Jell-O salads—we call them "Fluff"—thrill any room full of guests. My favorite? Picture a ginormous glass bowl with layers of crushed graham crackers, sliced bananas, and freshly whipped cream. Oh my ... the best!

Grandma remains passionate about reading. She claims she struggled with reading when she was a child, so she wanted her children to learn and love to read. She indeed passed that on as many of us share her passion.

And her sense of humor? Outstanding. She spills joy, and she wants to share it. Just thinking about the banter between Grandma and grandson Michael makes me smile. They just tease each other about all kinds of things. She helped us keep our sense of humor from being sucked away by darker times. Grateful for that, for sure.

Although their pace has slowed, Grandma Wanda and Grandpa Darrell still enjoy their friends, their family, their home. They are a huge reason I am finally sharing this work. I really wanted them to see the realization of this project where the shadow of the Almighty clearly overwhelms the shadow of death.

Reflections on the Interview

On January 13, 2007, I interviewed Grandma Wanda at her home in Wichita. Prior to the interview, she wrote multiple pages in her own handwriting along with filling out the initial project survey I sent, providing ease and prompts for the interview itself.

Lamp-lighting Perspective

The phone rang. I answered. Darrell and I were sitting with our grandchildren as our daughter and son-in-law were out for the evening.

"Hello? I'm sorry Steve and Lori are not home."

The caller stopped me. "Mom, this is Carlton." Our youngest son.

"Oh, I'm sorry. I didn't recognize your voice," I replied, a little confused.

"I'm not too surprised, Mom, because I have bad news."

And then, he said the unthinkable.

"Jamie's committed suicide."

Immediately, I shrieked. "Oh, no! Oh, no!" (I've felt bad about this as I imagine Carlton has replayed that over and over in his mind too many times.)

Darrell hurried to take the phone until I composed myself. Darrell continued to talk with Carlton. I remember asking, "How did he do it?" I remember Darrell talking a bit longer, then he prayed with him and hung up the phone. I remember calling a dear friend to ask her to call another mutual friend as well as our pastor. Our pastor called us as soon as he knew.

Our youngest daughter, Gretchen, and her husband, Roy, also lived in Wichita. That evening, Roy and Gretchen were at his mother's home for a birthday party. I called and told Gretchen. They left the party and came to Lori's home. Lori and Steve arrived shortly after. So many questions, yet so much silence still.

Of course, we were all in shock. I felt I must be strong for them. As we left their home that night to go back to our home, I prepared myself to break the news to my sister and her husband. They were staying with us as my sister had just received a heart transplant. I was caring for her until she was strong enough to return to her country home.

We called our eldest son, Dave, and his wife, Marie. Of course, we talked to Tim. We also called Darrell's brother, Dean, and his wife, Doris. We asked them to tell Grandma Hazel.

I remember finally going to bed that night exhausted. Wanting to sleep. Trying to sleep. Tense and tired. Where is the rest at a time like this? So many memories swirling.

Jamie was a lively little boy. As our first grandchild, he was both fun and extra special to us. He was brilliant. No, he really was. He read all the time. He thought things out real well, too. I remember playing games with him. He won easily without hardly trying. This frustrated his younger brother so much.

We did get some rest that night. The next morning, we faced many detailed arrangements so we could be with the family. Meals needed to be prepared for my sister as we did not know how long we would be gone. We called Carlton, who worked for a major airline, and he made arrangements for us to fly to Denver. Somehow it all came together—something to be thankful for—and we headed to the airport.

When we boarded the plane, I burst into tears. With my sister's tender physical state, I had not yet found a place quiet and alone enough. Whether I was ready or not, the tears spilled out right there.

The thought the Lord impressed upon me comes from Genesis 50:20: "You intended to harm me, but God intended it for good to accomplish what is now being done, the saving of many lives."

When we landed in Denver, Carlton met us at the airport. He grabbed me, and he held me. Silently. We stood there for a time. Suddenly, I began to realize more than the pain we all shared. I remember greeting Kathy and her mother when we arrived at the house. He was really gone.

Where do you begin to comfort a fractured family?

I remember we all got ready to go to church, where they had a Christian counselor for the church and the many youth who knew Jamie, including some who had been at the camp when he hung himself. Although still in shock, I remember thinking the time spent together like that was profitable. That was on Sunday. Jamie died the day before, early evening.

The following day, Monday, many more people came. Work needed to be done to accommodate visitors, so I just tried to keep busy, which gives the mind a bit of a rest.

On Tuesday, Darrell and I went with Carlton and Kathy to the funeral home to help with those details. Carlton and Kathy also had to go pick out a plot at the cemetery. I remember picking out his casket. Who would have ever thought I'd pick out a casket for one of our grandchildren?

The body arrived on Wednesday. The funeral home prepared the body for family viewing. We spent all afternoon at the mortuary.

The funeral was on Thursday, January 23, 1992. I cried, and I cried like I had never cried before. What a time. I felt sorry I couldn't be more of a help to my kids. I had never known grief to this extent before. By this time, I had already buried both my parents, but this was very different.

Why? Almost harder than losing Jamie has been watching Carlton and Kathy go through all this grief and knowing we can't do anything to make it better. Standing by ... helpless.

But, in the midst of it all, we got glimpses of the good.

The initial response from Carlton and Kathy's church, coworkers, and friends was outstanding. They brought in meals to serve twenty people every day leading up to the funeral. I've never seen such a creative outpouring of love and ministry. They brought in paper goods like Kleenex, toilet tissue, paper plates, napkins. And because so many young people were coming and going, people generously shared pop by the cases. They really understood that no one feels like shopping, and they thought of everything we might need. From this church, I learned to take these kinds of things to other families when they grieve. There is a time of such shock that these thoughtful, generous gestures really do help so much.

Darrell and I stayed another week after the funeral to help. We helped write thank you notes. Taking the time to say thank you reminded us how many people did so many things to help lighten this heavy burden. We cleaned as we could and did the laundry and just about anything we could think to do to help the family get back to a "normal" we already knew would never be completely the same with the obvious one forever missing.

Throughout it all, there was much searching for clues. Jamie wrote a lot of his thoughts down, so there were clues in notebooks, in letters, and his choice of music pointing to his struggle with depression. So many unanswered questions remain. A couple specific ones for me:

1. Was it really more than most teens go through trying to finding their niche?

2. What happened to him at the local public high school that caused him to cry and plead not to have to go back there?

One thing that really helped is nothing was held back. The family shared everything that was found. Someone even made copies of all his notes and letters, so we could have copies to read through when we were ready. This helped us sort through our questions as well as sort through his belongings. I am grateful for that.

Although we only saw him about once a year, he was our first grandchild, and we enjoyed him. We're thankful he was part of our lives for seventeen and a half years, and we hurt. But Carlton and Kathy, he was their firstborn and their home felt so different without him. I ached for them and the kids, Michael and Holly. Oh, how we prayed they'd each know the good out of this awful situation.

They went through the motions of living. Michael had his sports and so many friends who kept him occupied. Holly was younger and at home more. I was more worried about her as she seemed to not realize he really wasn't coming home. Initially, she seemed to have fun claiming the things of Jamie's she wanted. I am not criticizing her. Maybe the items helped her feel he wasn't so far away. I'm sharing to remind us that we do not all grieve the same or at the same time. I just think it took her a long time to reach the real acceptance of his absence and the real grieving process.

No two people sort through grief alike. We draw our strength from the Lord, and he comforts and guides us so personally. He brings the good out of everything. What do people ever do without him?

I know some need quiet solitude. I needed to be busy. Even with all the work to catch up on when I got home, I knew leaving the family and going home would not be easy. Immediately, I was back caring for my sister. What will this new normal really look like?

How grateful we were to our family and friends for their outpouring of support through cards, flowers, and phone calls. The first Sunday back, we arrived intentionally late to church that morning, and we left as the last song was sung. I wasn't sure I could handle talking with people just yet. We did go back to church that Sunday evening, and I was able to stay clear through. Peace, in bits, comes.

One outstanding feeling I could not shake? The constant concern for Carlton, Kathy, and the kids did not wane. I woke up thinking of them, went to bed thinking of them, and countless moments through-out the days wondering how they were adjusting. Would the pain and ache ever quiet?

We already had a trip scheduled to Denver for a college class reunion in February 1992, so we flew back out, and we stayed for a week again. While we were there, we joined a group therapy session for suicide survivors. We took the opportunity to express what was going on in our own processing, but we also came to realize how important it was to know we are not alone. Truly, most helpful.

One thing I want to share is that I have never been ashamed of Jamie or his final act. I know this used to be a very common response to suicide—family shame—but not for me. Rather, I've been open with other people partly because you want others to know they are not alone. Also, I will always be proud of him.

Jamie was sick. He saw no relief in sight. His dreams of playing ball and becoming a pilot at the Air Force Academy were shattered. I'm sure this added to his unnerving. While I know I don't understand it all, I'm still so very proud of Jamie.

He loved planes and cooking like his dad. He loved LEGOs. He could win at games without even trying. Truly, a brilliant young mind.

Often, those early months, songs, or down days could trigger tears for me, which was quite abnormal for my temperament. But I should not have been surprised. He's gone. Our family has forever changed.

We don't forget. In fact, we found the first year he was gone that we needed to do something in memory of him. I know some choose to keep fresh flowers on the gravestone, but we chose to do something different.

We chose to share what brought us the most comfort and strength through our grief. We bought Gideon Bibles in Jamie's memory every month. You know the Bibles placed in hotel and motel rooms? Knowing troubled souls might need some guidance and comfort, we prayed these Scriptures would speak life into minds battling depression and hearts in need of salvation.

The Scriptures and prayer for our family had been deeply important to us before Jamie's death; however, they became even more vital to us after. Drawing strength from the Lord gave us opportunity to love and to live beyond our capacity.

The resounding ache does quiet down some. We carry on with a deeper compassion for those around us. But normal never really feels normal again.

As months passed, after everything changed, our house needed some remodeling, so our mental and physical focus preoccupied us and lightened the press of heartache. We still miss Jamie, and we always will. And our concern for our whole family's response to his death remains.

A pastor at a funeral of a godly man who committed suicide once said, "God didn't call him home, but he welcomed him."

Some days we may feel sadder than others. Questions still arise. Does the hurt ever really go away? No, we do adjust to it. We wish Jamie would have had a longer, fuller life, yet we must remember we still have a life to live. Hopeful living is a gift and a choice.

At every family occasion, we always feel the missing, but I've felt we ought not overly focus on Jamie's absence at the holidays or at our other grandchildren's special events; otherwise, we let death overshadow the living. Whether we say anything or not, Jamie is always missed, yet we must also be careful to go on enjoying life without restraining one another with added guilt and unearthing grief.

We want to be there to "rejoice with those who rejoice, and mourn with those who mourn," as Paul reminds us in Romans 12:15. Not with divided hearts. Rather, we choose how we adjust, remember the dead, and encourage real living.

Has God used all this for good? I'm sure he has in countless ways we cannot see. I am grateful for the ways he's allowed us to see good. For example, one of our daughters, Gretchen, worked at a bookstore. When customers inquired after books on suicide, her colleagues referred to her. Her assistance helped them find what they were looking for, but more than that her compassion encouraged them as well.

Our other daughter, Lori, and I had the opportunity to share our experience losing Jamie at Wichita State several years ago. After we shared our story, several young people approached us with tears. They thanked us for being willing to talk on the subject. Several were grieving losses, including some whose families decided to pretend the suicide away. Acknowledging death is one thing, but accepting it was a suicide is another. This denial was much more common in the past; however, this class helped me realize it is still a common method of hiding from the truth. We must be able to talk about it.

I remember one telephone call we received from a man who didn't believe in God and whose son committed suicide. This man, clearly tormented, found no comfort anywhere. Up to that point, he chose to close himself off from God. I pray for him and others like him to be softened toward God through these times, not hardened all the more.

For me, searching the Scriptures brought great strength and perspective. At first, I thought only of Judas Iscariot as being the primary suicide of the Bible. However, as I studied more, I realized how many there were and how profoundly God used them in life and in death.

So, how does all this help us today? The choice is ours. Death cannot be undone. We can choose to be defeated daily because of how our lives have changed, or we can watch God use it for good. We can draw others to the Lord Jesus Christ by following Him and thanking Him without restraint, or we can become sullen, bitter, and envious of others we think are experiencing good fortune.

"Now may the God of peace who brought again from the dead our Lord Jesus, the great shepherd of the sheep, by the blood of the eternal covenant, equip you with everything good that you may do his will, working in us that is pleasing in his sight, through Jesus Christ, to whom be glory forever and ever. Amen."
Hebrews 13:20-21

Join my prayer: Lord, please use Jamie's life and death to bring honor to your name by displaying your comfort and goodness in personal ways that draws souls to you, and restore them with your joy and strength.

"He Reached Out to Me"

Ken, Maternal Grandfather

Brief Personal History

G randpa Ken grew up farming on his family homestead on the plains of southeast Wyoming in a small community settled by our Swedish immigrant ancestors. Born March 24, 1919, he was the third child (and second son) of Harry and Carrie Lundberg.

He was shaped by the life of a Great Plains farmer, a hardy endeavor for any soul. Short summers and long winters established the contented spirit, diligent work ethic, and rooted faith required for endurance. He learned from a young age how to grow things, sing harmony, write poetry, and he developed a love for basketball.

Grandpa Ken was as an ever-studying man. He missed an entire year of junior high when his father needed extra hands on the farm. When he went back to school, the public district acknowledged his maturity and capability, so he skipped the grade he missed and moved on with his original class.

As a member of the Greatest Generation, Grandpa Ken served in the Army Air Corps as a cargo pilot over "The Hump," a.k.a. the Himalayas. The *Casper (WY) Star-Tribune* featured him in a 2010 series and bound book on World War II veterans. Upon his return from service, he met and married Grandma Phyllis. They had four children, and the family was raised on the farm where Ken grew up. He took over the farming operation from his dad in the 1950s. Ken excelled in carpentry, constructing photo frames, quilt racks, tables, etc. He tackled larger projects as well, including home renovations.

As the family grew with grandchildren, he added onto the farmhouse several times. More bedrooms. Larger kitchen and mud room. Numerous windows brought in rays of natural light throughout the day while framing summer sunrises and whistling winter whiteouts.

While marvelous memories were made there, hard times were endured as well. On an autumn day in 1982, the family home of forty years burned to the ground. Combined with consecutive years of crops freezing in the ground, the hardships opened Ken and Phyllis to the idea of moving east for a season.

They moved to Leavenworth, Kansas, where Grandpa Ken landed work in the oil industry and delightedly served military families in the church and community.

Eventually, Grandpa Ken and Grandma Phyllis moved back to Wyoming to live out their final nine years on the family farm homesteaded by Ken's grandparents, Peter and Sophie Lundberg.

Kenneth R. Lundberg died March 29, 2013.

Reflections on the Interview

Conducted July 4, 1997, this was one of my first family interviews. Grandpa Ken thoughtfully participated and commended me for taking on this project to honor Jamie's memory, help others facing similar loss, and ultimately share hope. He sat quietly at times throughout the interview. While he had already come to grips with Jamie's absence and was reassured by enduring faith, he acknowledged sadness remains.

Lamp-lighting Perspective

"Grandpa, can I talk with you and Grandma a bit in the basement?"

Jamie asked me this question on his last visit to our home. It was Thanksgiving 1991. He had traveled with Tim, Karen, and Heidi to our home, joining our youngest son and his family who arrived earlier.

During the days prior to this request, we enjoyed the preparations, the celebration of Thanksgiving, and the hours of college football that followed. The house brims and brews when the kids and grandkids gather. The table expands so we can all circle around it together for three square meals. At breakfast—just after eating, while still sipping on coffee—we'd read the Bible, Our Daily Bread, and pray together.

Then we'd all find something to do. A project here. An errand there. Working together where we can and around each other otherwise.

As much as the hem and hum of activity warms our home, a few extra quieter moments are always welcome to me. But this invitation from our eldest grandson serves as a special unforgettable memory to me.

Teenagers don't often seek out time with their ol' grandpa.

But Jamie did that day.

I suppose we had an average grandfather-grandson relationship. Jamie lived on our homestead the first five years of his life. As a farmer, I worked the land from dawn to dusk six days a week. Whether in my workshop, chicken house, Quonset, barn, or coming in from the fields, I recall hearing and seeing Jamie—and Heidi, too. Those two couldn't have been any closer, I don't suppose.

After Carlton and Kathy moved off the farm, I remember Jamie (Michael and little Holly, too) growing up so fast between our visits. From what I heard, he was quite a good student. Active little guy. I remember him wresting for the school. He read a lot. He sure seemed to enjoy learning. It came easy to him, I think.

As he aged into a teenager, I remember noting I never saw him upset or agitated. His ability to articulate: clear. His ability to pass a football: exceptional. And his self-control was admirable beyond his years. Always in control of himself, mature, and well-spoken. Bright. Very bright.

Struggles for Jamie surfaced during his freshman year. First, I remember he had to get glasses. He had dreams of being a military pilot. Like his dad, he loved planes. The corrective lenses meant he was physically disqualified for the fighter jets. I flew planes during World War II, so I understood the draw to fly and the turbulence that sticks with you years after war's end.

Additional external struggles picked at him, too, at a large public school near Denver, Colorado, where he lived with his parents by that time. He endured difficulties during football season. (Later, we learned coaches and students were directly part of this.) Evidently, the struggles worsened over the school year. According to his mom (my daughter), his anxiety grew. By spring and summer, his grades began to slip. He begged not to go back to that school. For a kid who rarely complained, this surprised me, but I figured he and his folks would figure it out. Honoring authority can be a curious thing to navigate, particularly in cases when authority is misused.

From my understanding, the family thought Jamie's social needs outweighed his living with immediate family. The decision: He'd live with his uncle (our eldest son) deep in the mountains. This way, Jamie could have a fresh start and attend a smaller school.

My son's own daughters lived with their mother in the city. However, his house in the mountains was already home to several young people. Those residing in the home at the time were our son and his wife, a stepdaughter, a girl friend of hers as well as a boy friend of hers who had rough family situation. This is what Jamie joined. Some thought this would serve as an answer to the social friction of the big city school— instant social circle right there in the home. They all went to the same high school, where Jamie again joined the football team. This move offered hope of a new beginning. Evidently, it played out with far less optimism than Jamie had banked on.

The eventual inconsistencies of this patchwork family structure are exactly what he wanted to talk to us about that Thanksgiving weekend. We made our way down the stairs and sat down together. Jamie spoke calmly. He outlined unfair treatment he thought he received while living there that fall. (He would return to his parents' home to live before Christmas.) Characteristically Jamie, he spoke clearly. I didn't sense bitterness. In fact, I sensed his desire: peaceful resolution. But again, he felt that was unfairly beyond reach. He did not lambaste anyone. He simply shared.

> "The thorough integration of strength and sensitivity, of firmness and feeling, is rare."
> **Eugene Peterson**
> *Run with the Horses*

From the details he shared (which aren't necessary to repeat here), I certainly understood his concern. In general, Jamie said he carried the heaviest weight of chore responsibility within the home while the other teens either didn't have chores or got away easily without doing them. Also, Jamie explained that while all the teens in the home were at least sixteen years old and licensed drivers, Jamie was the only one not allowed to drive. When he attempted to seek explanation, he said he was silenced without reason.

In such a situation, I see how a young man's self-respect could easily erode, yet I certainly never imagined Jamie was in the process of giving up on living. He spoke clearly. Calmly. Compassionately. He really didn't want to burden others with the conflict. I think he hoped we'd help.

"Ask the former generation and find out what their
ancestors learned, for we were born only yesterday
and know nothing, and our days on earth are but a shadow.
Will they not instruct you and tell you? Will they not
bring forth words from their understanding?"
Job 8:8-10

In addition to this conflict, Jamie's dream of playing football deflated, as he did not get to play in any games in yet another season. In his big city high school, his slighter build in a sea of larger athletes hid his ability to strategize the game better than many men I know. He had hoped the smaller school, smaller team would offer a different outcome.

I'm told he practiced with drive and determination. Eagerness ... and asthma. He even practiced through asthma attacks pleading to be deemed worthy in the coaches' eyes. The harsh words—and probably that physical, health weakness—nearly ripped away his love for the sport.

Instead of gaining strength during the season, Jamie's health actually depleted. He lost weight. His asthma did not allow him to persevere and progress as hard as his will pushed. He was hospitalized at least once for his health directly related to these practices. I suppose altitude may have been a factor, too.

The coaches didn't play him, but I don't blame the coaches. He really hadn't been there long enough for them to know how serious or not-so-serious his asthma may have been.

But I certainly do feel for him. He loved football. He could throw the ball. And his thinking game ... bright. In the end, just so sad, really.

"Because he talked so little, his words had a peculiar force, they were not worn dull from constant use."
Willa Cather
My Ántonia

Our talk that day didn't last all that long. Jamie didn't belabor his points. He just wanted us to know what he thought. I am still not sure why he chose to share. Maybe seeking our help? Not sure we managed to do that, but I am thankful for that talk that day, that memory.

Our little Jamie ... a young gentleman, indeed.

On January 16, 1992, Kathy and her two younger children (Michael and Holly) came to visit for the long weekend. Jamie opted to attend a winter retreat with his church youth group.

Although we were a bit disappointed, we certainly understood and were a little hopeful he was making some good friends after the difficult couple years. Also, some suspected his interest in spiritual matters had dwindled in recent months, so his initiative to go on such a retreat was a welcome option.

The evening of January 18, 1992, the phone rang. I answered it. The voice on the other end? I didn't recognize his voice at first. Strained. Sensitive. Sad. Our son-in-law, Carlton. He spoke directly, matter of fact.

"Jamie killed himself."

Initially, I could not believe he would joke about something like that. But within moments, I knew this wasn't a joke. Jamie's gone. Shock set in immediately. I numbly told Phyllis and Kathy. Their tears. ... The screams ... shook the street, I think. Then, hearing the commotion, Michael and Holly rushed in.

"What's wrong?" I think they asked.

By now, I'm not even sure what explanation they received. A total blur in my memory. I remember Phyllis flew with Kathy and the kids while I drove from Kansas City to Denver the next day. The blur continued. I do not remember any part of that drive. Numb, I suppose.

As the family gathered for the funeral, we shared sorrow and loss. Jamie's gone. We proceeded through the customary funeral preparations. Trips to the funeral home and cemetery. No dress rehearsal. Nothing prepares you for all the formal finalities.

One thing I really regret now is that I viewed the body. I'd been to several funerals in my life, seen the bodies, and it didn't trouble me. However, Jamie's body ... in a coffin. That's different for me. Very hard to see. I wish I'd never seen it. And I can't seem to forget it either.

I want to remember the young gentleman from Thanksgiving instead. Sure, he had concerns, but he also seemed to be handling them with grace and peace ... maturity beyond his years.

Remembering Jamie ... some memories, I just want to be fresh again; others, just sad. What could I have done differently that may have impacted his decision? Or, if in fact, did I do anything that contributed to his decision? That troubles me some still.

I hurt for Kathy and Carlton and the family, a hurt I had not known before. If it were possible, I would have done just about anything to take that pain away. We cannot walk in another man's shoes even though we sure would like to sometimes.

Recalling memories of his childhood with Phyllis and Kathy eases grief's sting, I think. When he got excited as a toddler, he bent his elbows, clenched his fists, and then he'd swing his arms back and forth like he was running fast, but standing in place with the biggest grin on his face. The countless rides on the tractor or combine, his laugh—and Heidi's, too—laughs that I hushed from time to time. And what a proud big brother. A good brother, too.

Photographs around the house remind us of Jamie's life. His death is hard, but the manner of death is the hardest part. I think general knowledge of Scripture and trusting that God's children cannot be lost, that brings a great deal of comfort despite what Jamie did.

Prior to Jamie's death, I remember a childhood friend losing his life to his own hand. We never knew if it was an accident or on purpose, but you think about these things even if no one talks about them. Back when we were younger, you just didn't speak of such things.

Although I've not spoken all that much about Jamie's death, I'd be open to sharing with another going through a similar situation. We deal with any death. It takes time, but this kind of death has its own sharp, deep pain, too.

I think it is important to know that time does take the edge off. Accepting the absence of a grandson—first-born grandson—is not easy.

But I am thankful God gives us memories. We've got some real good ones with Jamie and the rest of the family, too.

God steadies us with his faithfulness, too. He builds a foundation of faith.

In our case, he used family for this, too, a strong heritage. He also gives us hope. Hope in Jesus.

"When darkness seems to hide his face, I rest on his unchanging grace."

Hope that leads us to heaven one day.

And I look forward to seeing Jamie there one day.

He reached out to me ... and I remember.

My hope is built on nothing less
Than Jesus' blood and righteousness.
I dare not trust the sweetest frame,
But wholly lean on Jesus' Name.

Refrain:
On Christ the solid rock I stand,
All other ground is sinking sand;
All other ground is sinking sand.

When darkness seems to hide his face,
I rest on his unchanging grace.
In every high and stormy gale,
My anchor holds within the veil. [Refrain]

His oath, his covenant, his blood,
Support me in the whelming flood.
When all around my soul gives way,
He then is all my hope and stay. [Refrain]

When he shall come with trumpet sound,
Oh may I then in him be found.
Dressed in his righteousness alone,
Faultless to stand before the throne. [Refrain]

Edward Mote
"My Hope is Built On Nothing Less" (1843)

Patios and Picnics

Phyllis, Maternal Grandmother

Brief Personal History

Grandma Phyllis was born September 18, 1927, in Momence, Illinois, the eldest child and only daughter of Philip and Ruth LaBue. She grew up in Chicago Heights, where she remembered her large Sicilian family gatherings with great fondness—usually involving bodies of water, fish fries, high-energy conversation, and laughter.

After graduating from high school, she moved with her family to a tiny little farming town in southeast Wyoming, where her dad served as local pastor. It was there she met Kenneth Lundberg as he returned from World War II. They married quickly, and remained married for sixty-seven years. They had four children, two sons bookending a pair of daughters: Karen (Heidi's mom) and Kathy (Jamie, Michael, and Holly's mom).

The three greatest loves of her life were her Lord, her family, and all things beautiful, from sunrises to purring kittens to strawberry patches, painting ceramics, and music. At an early age, Grandma Phyllis learned to play the piano and sang with her dad. Her love for music continued throughout her life. As an active member of her local choir, she enjoyed singing solos, duets, and quartets.

She read her Bible and prayed for her family and loved ones daily. She enjoyed women's luncheons. She also dutifully prepared and served many meals to farmers and harvesters in their home. She lit up every room she walked in and delighted to love anyone in her path.

She was an accomplished seamstress and excelled in ceramics. She also owned her own shop, Phyllis' Ceramic Den. She exercised an exceptional ability to paint life-like eyes.

Among many challenges (see Ken's history section for more of their shared hardships), Grandma Phyllis also suffered migraines nearly her entire life.

Phyllis Nancy LaBue Lundberg died September 1, 2013.

Reflections on the Interview

Conducted July 4, 1997, this was one of my first family interviews. Grandma Phyllis eagerly participated, answered my questions thought fully, and commended me several times for taking on this project to honor Jamie's memory and help others facing similar loss. She cried at several points and delighted to remember Jamie as her little cowboy on the farm when he lived near. While she had already come to grips with his absence, she remained unsettled with what had gone so terribly wrong for him to sink into such hopelessness.

Lamp-lighting Perspective

Before we moved to Leavenworth, Kansas, my husband Ken and I lived on our farm in western Nebraska along the Wyoming border for over forty years. Ken's dad and grandad farmed the land. After the Second World War, Ken returned to the prairie after serving as a pilot in Asia for the United States Army Air Corps. Although he was nine years older than me, we met, married, and settled into farm life within six months. He was twenty-seven, and I was eighteen years old. We were oh-so-blessed to raise our family on the farm.

Our daughters met their husbands when the young brothers, Tim and Carlton, were part of a traveling harvest crew assisting farmers. The crews would start as far south as Texas and work their way north to assist farmers in the harvesting process throughout the summer months. These two young men from Wichita, Kansas, loved the country. Farming is tough work, but both young men loved the challenge and adventure in the summer during their high school years.

After graduating high school in the spring of 1969, Karen and Tim went to John Brown University in Siloam Springs, Arkansas, that fall. Tim proposed that winter. They married in July of 1971 and lived in Siloam Springs until graduation. Carlton and Kathy married in August of 1972 following their graduation from high school the previous May.

Of course, we were thrilled to have Carlton and Kathy living on our farm soon after they married. They lived a short time in Wichita immediately following their wedding. Soon they moved near us and lived in one of the houses on our home-place.

Following Tim's graduation from JBU in 1974, he and Karen moved to a place three miles away in southeast Wyoming. When our first grandson, Carlton Jamison Plinsky, was born, we were completely overjoyed. From the beginning, he was a simply delightfully happy baby. With that little guy living right next door, we got to see him every single day for the first five years of his little life. What a joy! Now and then, he would ask or we would invite him to spend a night in our home. I can still see him teetering on the sidewalk that connected our two houses with that big suitcase. He tried so intently to balance himself. What a sight, that little guy!

When Jamie was about three years old, he was visiting our house as I was soaking my feet in a tub of hot water. (This was a method of relaxation for a farmer's wife. I spent much of my day in the garden or standing in the kitchen preparing meals for lots of hungry mouths ready to eat between hours of farming in the summer sun.) Jamie decided he wanted to join me, so he pulled up a chair next to me. He climbed into the chair and plopped his feet into the water. Instantly, he pulled his feet out of the water. With wide eyes, he proclaimed, "Dumb kid!" Oh, how I loved and laughed with that little boy!

He and Heidi roamed and played and "worked" alongside all of us in those days. Sometimes they helped me weed and pick strawberries in my strawberry patch as I clipped laundry to dry on the line. Then I'd let them sit on the patio and enjoy snacking on their harvest. Those two were something else. A little ornery. So sweet and silly. And quite well behaved and mannered most of the time. Jamie ... such a happy boy.

Having Carlton, Kathy, and Jamie, then later Michael, live on the farm with us was such a blessing! They were such a part of our daily life. And we were a part of theirs, too.

Once, when several friends and family had gathered for a meal and some fellowship, Jamie began to choke on a steak bone. His grandpa (my Ken) grabbed him out of his high chair and dislodged the bone. Jamie did not seem fazed, but he sure scared the rest of us that day.

> *"The LORD is my shepherd; I shall not want. He maketh me to lie
> down in green pastures: he leadeth me beside the still waters."*
> **Psalm 23:1-2 (KJV)**

Personally, I relished the time with Jamie and Heidi as their first Sunday School teacher in our little community church in Albin, Wyoming. I helped them memorize the 23rd Psalm. What a sweet time to watch our grandchildren, who looked so much like twins, come dressed in their "Sunday best," interacting with one another. Oh, how I treasure those memories!

The springtime before Jamie was to begin kindergarten, his parents decided to move so his dad could take a job about six hours away in central Nebraska. We did not realize how much we would miss them until our homestead lost the daily hustle of Jamie and Michael (who joined the family just a year earlier).

Sadly, from then on we did not get to see Jamie's family as often as I would have liked. With Carlton's work and the operations of our own farm, we only got to see them three or four times a year. How those kids grew between visits! We did keep in contact by following the children's academic progress closely as well as activities like wrestling or church plays in which they were involved. We visited them as often as we could.

Our whole family enjoyed following football, especially the University of Nebraska and the Dallas Cowboys. I enjoyed shopping for the boys, often choosing football memorabilia. Football, our weekend entertainment and a great connector for our family, gathered us all around the television. Some slipped into naps, but not Jamie. Jamie loved football, and he really understood the game. And he was so smart. Ken always said, "He's going to be a quarterback!" Later, when Carlton moved his family to Colorado, Jamie organized football games in the street.

Another fascination for Jamie living in the big city was the ability to see the airplanes. He shared the love for aviation with his dad. Carlton loves planes. Working for an airline, he was able to take his family on many plane trips. Those boys could tell you so much about all types of planes from military to commercial. We knew Jamie's dream to become a fighter pilot. His grandpa had served his country during the war as a pilot, so this was something we also anticipated with him. We remember when he received the news from his doctor that he needed glasses. Most children would have been excited for the novelty. Jamie? Devastated. He knew the military academies would see him unfit for flight school with such a handicap. That was his freshman year in high school.

"He restoreth my soul: he leadeth me in the paths of righteousness for his name's sake. Yea, though I walk through the valley of the shadow of death, I will fear no evil: for thou art with me; thy rod and thy staff they comfort me. Thou preparest a table before me in the presence of mine enemies: thou anointest my head with oil; my cup runneth over."
Psalm 23:3-5 (KJV)

What a tough year that was for him! He had been so excited about going to high school to join a real football team. He bought the uniform, he memorized plays, and he practiced with all his heart. He did not get to play even a minute of a game the entire season. This crushed him.

From that time on, Jamie seemed to carry a sadness with him. Our loving and happy little boy grew discouraged. Some young people do not have specific dreams or goals, but Jamie did. Yet they all seemed to unravel one after the other when he entered high school.

He did not lose his sense of humor entirely, but he became more serious more of the time. I remember the last time he visited our home, Thanksgiving 1991. I had some photos for Kathy, so I took them to Jamie. When I asked him to slide them into his suitcase, he looked at me with his half-smile and said, "I don't have room, Grandma!" We giggled, and he packed the photos neatly into his duffel bag.

"Surely goodness and mercy shall follow me all the days of my life: and I will dwell in the house of the LORD forever."
Psalm 23:6 (KJV)

On that same visit, we noticed Jamie's maturity. He wanted to talk with Grandpa and me about his troubles living in the mountains. We went downstairs, and he calmly shared his concerns. Basically, three teenagers living together under one roof with different rules seemed unfair to him. If I would have been in the place he described, I would have been unhappy, too. One example: he was required to make his bed daily; the others did not. The others had permission to drive while Jamie did not. If there had been a reason, maybe he could have understood, but no reason had been given. Inconsistency is tough for anyone to swallow, but I think this is especially tough on teenagers.

Jamie lived up there because of an unsettling situation at his local public high school. Going to a smaller community might help. He originally looked forward to the change. However, I also remember him saying something about the one-year-old girl Kathy babysat at the time he moved out: "Rachel isn't going to remember me." He loved children, and he had often helped in the church nursery. We knew he was going to make a great daddy someday.

On the evening of January 18, 1992, I was playing a game of Aggravation with Michael and Holly. When the phone rang, I answered. The party on the line said, "Is Ken there?" I answered, "Yes, one minute." As I walked back to the bedroom to hand him the phone, I wondered who was calling. I didn't even recognize the voice of my own son-in-law, Carlton.

When Ken hung up the phone, I went back to see who had called. He said simply, "It's Jamie. He's gone!"

Instantly, I collapsed on the bed and started screaming. Kathy responded in turn, and Michael and Holly, too. My emotions controlled my body; however, I do remember seeing Kathy sitting on the edge of the bed shaking terribly.

In the days and weeks ahead, we hurt some for ourselves but more so for Kathy and Carlton. This kind of loss is so devastating!

I felt plagued by the unanswered questions. When someone close to you passes away—regardless of how—it hurts, but then especially in this way. What could have been so bad for him? Something horrible must have happened! Why couldn't Jamie have told someone? Why couldn't we have had the chance to help?

As I flew with Kathy and the children to Colorado, I felt we must hurry because Carlton was still alone. No family was present with him. I remember feeling so concerned about Carlton being alone. I remember seeing him so drained as he tried to explain what he knew and field our many questions.

We spent the week preparing for the funeral with many people coming and going with meals, snacks, and supplies as well as plants, flowers, and cards. Young people from the church Jamie and Michael's age lingered in the home for many hours. As I cried through much of this, I kept thinking, "Look at this ... look at this ... look at this. How could Jamie not have known how much he was loved?"

I think Jamie, with his heart of excellence and service, knew how to give to others. However, he had a real hard time receiving. Maybe he thought he was taking something, and he just could not do it. I don't know, but my heart still breaks thinking of this.

As I am of Italian ancestry (my grandparents emigrated from Sicily just before my dad was born), I am emotional. I cried so often in the months following, but I felt deep concern for Carlton and Kathy, Michael and Holly. Somehow, their little home would feel so empty, and I ached for them.

Also, my folks, Grandpa Philip and Grandma Ruth, were older and physically weaker. Emotionally, they seemed quite unsettled for a long time. My dad was an extremely sensitive man. I saw grand displays of his every emotion. Even when he knew one of his family was sick with a cold or the flu, he would get upset to the point of tears at times, so I knew this would be nearly unbearable for him and my mom.

Finally, I felt so concerned about Heidi. She and Jamie were like our twins. They had been so close. What is she going to do? How is she going to handle this?

While my own pain was deep and real, I felt a great deal of comfort just gathering with family those initial weeks and with church friends when we returned home. Our church friends comforted us with listening ears, wonderful meals, encouraging prayers, cards, and plants.

For me, crying myself and comfort from others drained much of the heaviness of the pain, but the deep confusion that followed still haunts me. I still can't believe he is gone. At times, I have felt so angry he hurt so much—from his mouth sores to the lack of sleep to the rejection of his freshman year. Why did this loving boy who was becoming such a wonderful young man have to endure so much pain so early in this life?

The Scripture from Ecclesiastes 3 shared at the funeral, "a time for everything," has been an encouragement to me. In a fallen world, we do have a time for birth and death, planting and harvesting, war and peace, laughter and tears, silence and speech. I still cannot claim to understand all this, but I trust the Lord will one day restore our fallen world.

Jamie's personal profession of faith in Jesus and baptism at age thirteen along with the Scripture where Jesus said, "let the little ones come unto me," comfort me. Despite Jamie's earthly suffering, he knew Jesus. Trusting in this truth, I have confidence Jamie is at eternal peace.

Our home continues to be filled with family photos, including Jamie. Often, I will pass one of his photos and think, "Where would you be now, Jamie? Would you be married like Heidi? Would you be an airline pilot? Would you be a dad?" The questions don't go away completely, but I am not overwhelmed by them.

Jamie sent a card to Ken, his grandpa, I treasure. In his handwriting, he signed it, "I love you, Jamie." What a gift for us to pick up every now and then! We loved him; he loved us. Oh, how I wish that could have been enough to keep him alive.

Even now, I cannot believe he is no longer with us. I can still see him on Grandma Ruth's patio on a midday picnic with Heidi—both her arms around his neck, Jamie smiling and pulling away.

What Are You Supposed to Do at Times Like This?

Carlton, Father

Brief Personal History

Carlton was the third and middle child born to Darrell and Wanda Plinsky. He has two older brothers and two younger sisters. He met Kathy while they were still in high school, and they married at age nineteen.

Carlton and Kathy had three kids: Jamie, Michael, and Holly. Carlton and Kathy's marriage dissolved in divorce after thirty-four years. Both Michael and Holly graduated college and married their spouses before this. Neither Kathy nor Carlton blame Jamie's death for this decision. Though they have gone their separate ways, both still visit Jamie's gravesite from time to time. They have not seen each other in years. The divorce occurred well after our 1999 oral interview.

Carlton's career has focused primarily in agriculture and aviation. He enjoys creatively cooking, gardening, reading, traveling, and the outdoors. Mountain biking, motorcycles, and rodeos are also favorite pastimes.

Reflections on the Interview

I interviewed my Uncle Carlton June 9, 1999, during my visit to celebrate Holly's high school graduation. He thoughtfully responded to my questions. Quietly. Pausing from time to time. He shared clearly and honestly. He communicated that he hoped sharing this would be helpful to others who find themselves on this hard road. Obviously, he did not wish for anyone to need this, but based on his experience with Jamie and sadly several others since, he knows it is a real road some must travel. He, too, does not want anyone to feel like they are alone in this grief.

Lamp-lighting Perspective

> "A man's mind vagued up a little, for how can you remember the feel of pleasure or pain or choking emotion? You can remember only that you had them."
> **John Steinbeck**
> *East of Eden*

"Oh, I don't know." The one thing I knew after Jamie's death. A dad bears burdens every day for his family. A choice and a duty. But, now? "I just don't know."

Jamie made me a dad when I was just twenty-one years old. Back in those days, dads were not allowed in the delivery room. Kathy went into labor just as a *Monday Night Football* game began. Jamie was born before the game was over. I have enjoyed football and the game's details for years; I do not remember much from that game at all.

I remember seeing Jamie for the first time, healthy and alive. I remember he rolled over the day we brought him home. We couldn't believe it. He also began sleeping through the night when he was still real young.

Jamie was a happy little guy. Bright blue eyes. Big smile. Easy to have around. Obedient and easy to teach. I remember potty training him at the farm. Outside seemed like the best place, so that's where he learned until Tim told me he didn't think this was a good idea with Heidi around so much. I adjusted for Heidi.

It was nice those two—Jamie and Heidi—grew up together. It was fun to watch them smile, make each other laugh, and grow up so close together.

As Jamie's dad (and Michael and Holly's, too), I saw myself as the primary/sole provider for the family. Devoted work was my duty, a discipline and decency I did without question. During some seasons, we lived on Kathy's folks' family farm, while other seasons took us to Kansas, Nebraska, the mountains of Colorado, and finally Denver.

Eventually, though we loved country living, we realized the city offered reliable job opportunities. I worked agricultural and builder-related jobs before I found my career with a major airline. I worked long hours and late shifts through the kids' growing up years.

Our times together were limited. We did enjoy daily meals together. I often made meals, too. I enjoy the experimentation of cooking. One fun thing I did from time to time was put food coloring in potatoes for Christmas or St. Patrick's Day.

Yes, I worked quite a bit, but we also enjoyed the perks of flying. Back then, our employee standby passes only cost us taxes to fly. I enjoyed taking the family on several vacations, including several to Hawaii, as well as providing the passes so family could fly places without me, too.

We moved to Nebraska when Jamie was about to start kindergarten. His August birthday gave us the choice as to when he should begin his formal education. We decided to enroll him the year he would be on the older end of the class roster. He was already reading, so we felt good about his preparedness to begin school later. However, as he got older, he became more and more bored with regular classroom work. He was enrolled in gifted and talented programs that helped some until he went to high school.

Athletically, Jamie loved sports. He loved to play them. He was exceptional at strategizing, especially in football. He went out for the high school team as a freshman. He was so looking forward to finally playing the game he watched on television most Saturdays (Cornhuskers) and Sundays (Broncos).

Not long into the season, I realized the football program was not teaching fundamentals of the game. Rather, they expected the boys to know the terms, the notes, and expected perfect execution. Jamie did his best, but he grew more and more discouraged. I quietly showed up at a few practices to see how Jamie was doing. His work ethic was clear. He was still a bit tentative. His endurance was strengthening. Yet he did stand off to the side of the team some.

I guess he was not aggressive enough for the coaches. They did not play him even a minute of any game—including one where they were far ahead. Sadly, before the season ended, Jamie asked to quit. Of course, we said no. "You can't just quit." I remember thinking one day he will understand how important perseverance is and how we cannot take on a quitting mindset. Just not right.

I did worry he might get hurt during practice because of his hesitancy at times—too tentative to get in there as aggressive football requires. I remember his final game; Jamie quietly rebelled. He chose not to suit up. I noticed, but I did not say anything. Not sure the coaches even noticed.

Jamie really did not show a big change in personality around me. I never saw him overly emotional. With football, though, I knew he was disappointed. He had so wanted to play. He tried his best. I am sure the coaches were not trying to beat him down. I do think Jamie never fully recovered from that disappointing season.

Between the football fiasco and begging not to return to the public high school he'd attended, I could see why he would like to return to the small town school in the mountains he had attended in fifth grade. His education was the most important priority to me, but I also understood the social pressures could interfere with gaining that education.

So when Kathy and Jamie suggested he spend the summer in the mountains, it made sense to me. Summer reached into his junior year, and he transferred to the school up there. I did not picture his high school years like this, but if it helped him develop and focus on education, I would not fight it.

When Jamie returned to our home before completion of fall semester, I was glad to have him home. I thought it might take time for him to transition. With determination, he insisted to go to a small private school. I worked to make that happen, too.

Jamie often waited up late for me to get home from work. We talked sports, about the day—the average stuff, I suppose. The last time I saw him was around noon or so the day he left for camp. I was packing up for work. He was packing for the retreat.

I hollered up to him, "Have fun."

He responded.

That was it.

A favorite memory of Jamie was the night before. We had been setting up his room so he could paint it, moved furniture so the walls were more easily reachable. I stopped by his room that night. We talked about music from my era and his. Ordinary maybe. The ease of our interaction that evening was just a normal night for a dad and his firstborn son, a son who had been through a lot. But that night I saw maturity, responsibility, and a real good kid.

Jamie listened to metal music. I didn't like it. We told him we didn't like it. I am sure it did not help his hidden depressive thinking, but whatever was troubling him went beyond the music.

I had limited exposure to suicide before Jamie. A guy from work had died by suicide a year or so before, as did a friend's child in his twenties. I figured a couple things about a person who did that. First, they had to be brave to carry it through, and things must be real bad for them to see that as the only option—the final solution.

On January 18, 1992, I received a phone call at work from the pastor's wife instructing me to call the camp due to an "emergency." I called the camp. They gave me another phone number to call. So, I hung up and called the next number. The guy who answered the phone simply and abruptly stated, "Jamie hung himself."

"Is he dead?" I asked.

"A doctor is attending to him. Somebody's been working on him for about an hour. They thought they got a faint heartbeat, but nothing in the past half hour or so."

Life Flight was still quite a ways from the remote mountain camp. He asked what I thought we should do. They needed permission to stop. Since I was not there or anywhere close, I just said, "Let the doctor decide." I knew he knew more than I did. I was shocked. Stunned.

My first action upon hanging up the phone at work? I kicked a chair across the room. I couldn't really speak for a few minutes. A guy made some comment about the flying chair as I exited the big room into the hall. Slumping against the wall, I had no clue what to do next. Thinking ... I'm on duty at work. My son just died. I'm hours away. What are you supposed to do at times like this? Never been so confused in my life.

Fortunately, a union representative walked down the hall. I called him over. Somehow I told him enough for him to kick in to help me figure out how to officially check out of my shift. He did all the talking for me. This was such a help. He may never know how much he helped me that night. He even took me to the parking lot and made sure I was okay to drive home. That is exactly what I did. Barely remember that drive.

When I walked into the quiet house, I wondered what to do next. I needed to make the calls. I remember calling my parents' home, but they were at my sister's house that night. My aunt, who was recovering from heart surgery at my folks' place, answered the phone. I just told her straight. Later hoped I didn't cause her extra stress.

I got ahold of my dad. I told him. I called my in-laws' home. Phyllis answered. I hoped Ken would answer, so I just asked for him. I felt it was probably best for him to tell Kathy and the kids in person.

Pastor called and came over. He helped me figure out if I'd have to identify the body. We did not, but we decided to drive to camp right away anyway.

We spent about fifteen minutes or so with the sheriff to pick up Jamie's athletic bag, glasses, Walkman, and personal belongings they collected. I remember how hard the sheriff took telling me the news. He told me he, too, had a seventeen-year-old son at home. I guess we both knew how turbulent teen years can be, and this is the absolute worst outcome.

Pastor and I ended up at the camp. The camp was low-key and dark by the time we arrived. We went to the dining hall, where we found our friend Roger, a youth director. He was taking it pretty hard. I think he was concerned about how I'd react to seeing him.

"How are you doing?" he asked.

My immediate response was, "Probably better than you." I meant it. I figured all he saw and endured must have been horrible. I felt for him. I felt for all of them: the campers, the other counselors.

They had emptied most of the lodge building where Jamie died, so they gave us bunks to stay in a room just across the way from where Jamie breathed his last. I was concerned Pastor needed to get back for church, but I am really glad we got some rest that night. I actually slept for a bit before we had to leave just before dawn.

After returning to Denver, our friend Johnny took us to the airport so we could pick up Kathy, her mom, and kids who caught an early flight back. We arrived early enough for me to check the computer at work.

As I was in the workspace, a coworker approached and said, "I thought you committed suicide."

"Wait ... what?" I thought. I asked him to repeat what he said. I must have heard him wrong. No, he said it again. This time he added something about the Nebraska Cornhuskers recent loss. The once-common cliché cut straight to my already quivering heart.

We don't realize how many jokes reference death and suicide until we experience a core-cutting loss. I know he didn't mean harm from what he said. I also know I'll never joke about those kinds of things again. You never know what people are facing. I do not want to pour salt into already open or hidden wounds.

When Kathy's plane arrived, we met at the gate. They disembarked, all of us still in shock and so tired. Teary-eyed, we quietly circled and hugged and went home.

When I went into Jamie's room for the first time, it was really strange. Fresh paint brushed and rolled by my boy when he was still alive—paint still fresh, but my boy was not even going to be here again. It struck. Heavy. Hollow.

My mind kept trying to understand. When an older person dies, we grieve their presence in our lives, but we recognize a life lived and the hope of heaven. How do you wrap your mind around a seventeen-year-old son with the world full of potential in front of him taking his own life? One second, there painting his room; the next, stilled and gone. Gone forever.

One of the things I remember most from those first few days is feeling physically full, like I had just eaten a whole meal. For Saturday until Monday or Tuesday, people kept offering food. I just could not eat. I finally ate because I woke up to such a horrible headache. I ate a small sandwich and felt full again.

I remember wondering: How do you even find a funeral home? Thankfully, someone from church gave us a contact. Our whole church seemed to mobilize. In those early days, they did a great job with meals, cards, and overwhelming kindness.

We had from January eighteenth to the twenty-third from death to funeral, a no-man's-land of sorts. As more people came, I eased into taking things day to day. One step at a time was about all you can handle.

The airlines and my coworkers were kind to give me time off. They eventually even let me change shifts for a while. An employee dropped off a case of soda because they heard our house was full of teenagers and kids. I remember thinking how good it was to have people of all ages squeezing in to huddle together remembering Jamie. You hear stories you've never heard before, and it feels good to know all those people knew and loved my boy.

I remember the shower head broke that week, so I had to replace that. Under unfathomable circumstances, things still happen reminding you regular life is still there somehow.

I remember some crying and a whole lot of laughing that week. Crying does not bother me. You expect some people to do a lot of it. It just shows his death affected people. Some who did not cry made you wonder a little, too. And the laughing: a welcome yet somewhat awkward expression. Remembering the good times—so many good times—makes you wonder why Jamie could not see how much he was loved by so many. I also remember people stopping by, and people were laughing. I figured it was awkward for them too. And confusing.

That last year of Jamie's life was a whirlwind of change. We had gone to a graduation for a step-nephew back in a mountain town we'd lived briefly a few years back. Jamie asked, "Why can't we live here again?" He wanted out of the city. We let him summer up there. Then he stayed for nearly all of first semester. He faced conflict. He had stood up for himself. He wanted to come home. I was glad he was home.

I could not begin to imagine what would unfold just a few weeks after his return. He spent Thanksgiving with Heidi. Next, Christmas. Then his wisdom teeth pulled. He was just getting his energy back from that rough procedure ... when he painted his room.

Jamie's body traveled to Pueblo before coming off the mountains. Since it was a holiday weekend, there was a delay. The funeral home prepared his body for viewing. I did not want to see his body ... without him. But you know you got to do it even though it was hard.

When the funeral directors guided us to the room, I did not want to go in there. I did not want to look. When I did, it did not look much like him to me. His hairline and hairstyle looked off to me. His shirt collar was positioned right under his chin. I hear it is not easy to reassemble after an autopsy. Maybe they can't get the physical back the same, but the truth is nothing will ever be the same. Viewing the body forces you to see, to accept what really happened.

I did not look at his hidden wounds. I know some did. It did not bother me at all to see some gently sliding his collar down because they may have needed to see it to accept it. I just did not need more evidence. My son was gone. I knew it.

The funeral was tough but good. So many people. Overflow rooms. Songs and sadness. Stories of Jamie's character of kindness, brilliance, dreams, and service shared. Snow. Sunlight. Red and white balloons released at the graveside. Cold, calm, comforting—yet also started the quiet and the confusion to come.

As family traveled back to their homes, we stayed back at home, but home felt hollow and heavy. Three or four weeks after Jamie died, we began attending a grief support group specifically for families who were grieving loss to suicide. At first, I remember feeling concerned because, you know, only nutty people's kids die like this. Before we walked in there, I kept wondering what kind of wacko people would be in there. Just walking in was hard the first time.

What I found? A surprising group of really nice, good people. As they shared their stories, I related and felt for them. They did not make us share Jamie's story the first night, which was a relief. I did not look forward to that.

What I found comforting with the support group was I did not need to worry about talking about suicide because these people all knew. Listening does help. Listening to parents who were three to six months ahead of us was very helpful to me. Making small progress like sleeping better, less confusion and indecisiveness, and a general lightening—as small as it may be—was evidence to me of taming grief.

I do not enjoy answering questions in a large group in general, so this applied to this group too. But I did participate. And I enjoyed one-on-one or small group conversations before and after the group meetings as well. Those few hours each week served as a safe place of comfort and were even a little relaxing.

Resuming any kind of routine was tough. I went from working nights to bereavement leave to working days. I remember enjoying reviewing the sports page in the mornings for years. Then Jamie joined me—such a mind for sports. I just could not bring myself back to the sports page alone.

I remember feeling the weight of previously normal responsibilities. I found making decisions extra difficult. I had to reevaluate everything. What is most important?

For six months, I worked the day shift. I did not want any extra responsibilities at work. I wanted to be able to do my job well. I knew I could not handle any more responsibility. I went to work and went home as quietly as I could. If I had been offered a lead position then, I just could not have done it at that time. I'm thankful it came later.

As Michael and Holly grew up and spent more time with friends or at school activities, I remember worrying about where they were if they were just a little late coming home—a kind of worry intensified because now you understand that worst fears can and do happen. You do not expect it to happen to your kids ... until it does. I think Michael eventually understood. I think I was a little hard on him.

A guy at work once said, "I don't know how you do it." My response? Coming back to work is just something you got to do. Putting it off isn't going to help anything.

I only knew a couple people who died by suicide before Jamie but dozens or more after, including several from work. I remember a coworker died by suicide. His shift overlapped mine. A real nice, outgoing guy, everyone liked him. One day, he was there working alongside all of us. Then he was gone, another suicide statistic. We were shocked. Again.

Several coworkers started talking to me about him. I will always be open to talk to anyone who wants or needs to talk about this kind of death and the grief that follows, though I will rarely speak of it first. I firmly believe it is a subject people should talk about if they need to, and I will not avoid those conversations.

I remember several coworkers asking questions. They kept saying, "I can't see how you can deal with this." Somewhere along the way, I learned the stages of grief. I think I felt all of them but shame and blame. I've never felt shame for Jamie or myself, but the other ones? I felt them, sometimes within minutes of each other. Recognizing what feelings surface is helpful. We do not have to get stuck in emotions when we simply recognize them.

I love my kids. I loved Jamie. Jamie died by suicide. Feeling his absence hurts. Living with his absence is hard. This is to be expected because of the love. I try to remember that.

I know some want to figure out a reason. A reason may include blaming someone. I did not really go through that maze. I figured going down that road at all was not worth the effort. It would not bring Jamie back. At this point, it is too late. Sure, you wonder if there were direct causes to his final decision, but I don't think knowing would make me feel any better.

I think we sometimes fear we will forget. Like life will go on in some way, and we'll forget. But we had seventeen years of memories, a lot of real good ones, that we don't forget. I think eventually living with the grief gets better, easier, but life is not the same. We can actively remember the good times.

One way I chose to carry Jamie's memory into my present days includes my plants. One of the plant arrangements given to us the week Jamie died included four plants that I have tended, transplanted into their own planter, and just let grow ever since. I have always enjoyed farming and gardening, so this was a natural way for me to make space to both mark time and to observe and appreciate fresh growth. One plant reaches six feet now.

From Beginning to End
Kathy, Mother

Brief Personal History

Kathy was the third of four children born to Ken and Phyllis Lundberg. She met Carlton while they were still in high school, and they married at age nineteen.

Kathy and Carlton had three kids: Jamie, Michael, and Holly. The marriage dissolved in divorce after thirty-four years. Both Michael and Holly graduated college and married their spouses before this. Neither Kathy nor Carlton blame Jamie's death for this decision. Though they have gone their separate ways, both still visit Jamie's gravesite from time to time. They have not seen each other in years. The divorce occurred well after our 1999 oral interview.

Kathy describes herself as friendly, organized, and emotional. She was a full-time homemaker, wife, and mother who enjoys playing piano, cross-stitching projects, and reading books.

Reflections on the Interview

I interviewed my Aunt Kathy on June 9, 1999, during my visit to celebrate Holly's high school graduation. The interview took place in the room that had been Jamie's at the family home in Aurora, Colorado, a suburb of Denver.

Lamp-lighting Perspective

"There is a time for everything,
and a season for every activity under the heavens ..."
Ecclesiastes 3:1

Carlton Jamison Plinsky (Jamie) made us proud, first-time parents on August 26, 1974. Carlton and I were young, both twenty-one years old when Jamie was born. We enjoyed the wonders of our first pregnancy, a surprisingly easy one. Along with our own anticipation, we enjoyed knowing Tim (Carlton's brother) and Karen (my sister) were also expecting their only child (Heidi) to be born in October. This was back before gender reveals and customary ultrasounds. Carlton and I lived on my parents' farm; Tim and Karen had made their home just a few miles down the road.

"A time to embrace ..."
Ecclesiastes 3:5

Jamie, with bright blue eyes, was a smiley baby. With Karen so close, Jamie and Heidi spent a lot of time together. Even in those early months, the two often shared a crib for naptime. From the beginning, they seemed to be at ease and often enamored with one another.

I remember when they first discovered their hands. We were overjoyed to watch them steady their reach and touch each other's face so gently. They made each other smile and giggle. Maybe since they were our first and only children up to that point, time seemed to stand still with them. I still remember so many vivid moments of those two when they were so little. Such sweet memories.

> "As I went back alone over that familiar road, I could almost believe that a boy and girl ran along beside me, as our shadows used to do, laughing and whispering to each other ..."
> **Willa Cather**
> *My Ántonia*

As toddlers, Jamie and Heidi were inseparable. Our home on my parents' place was near two other houses. My parents lived in one, and my grandparents summered in one. The two children took turns going back and forth among the houses. Watching from windows, we saw them chasing each other. Maybe Heidi first, but then Jamie, too, as if they took up the game of tag before we even taught them. They climbed the propane tank and enjoyed sliding down. As active as they were, sometimes we would find them sitting on the sidewalk playing in the dirt.

Jamie and Heidi loved playing outside together all year long. Wyoming winters required we bundle them up as they toddled about in the winds and blowing snow. During the summers, they spent many daylight hours as well as many evenings with Grandpa Philip and Grandma Ruth, their great-grandparents who summered in Wyoming and wintered in the south.

In the months leading up to the birth of our second child, Michael (who was born in 1978 when Jamie was three), Jamie repetitively told people at church or those who came to the farm, "Our baby is coming." When we brought Michael home, Jamie insisted he hold his little brother "all by myself; no one help me!" Jamie seemed to not only adjust well to Michael joining our family, but he also took proud ownership of him too. Jamie and Heidi confessed years later they would sneak into the nursery to pinch Michael while he was napping. We had no idea.

Although Jamie's birthday made him eligible to begin kindergarten in the fall of 1979, we opted to keep him home one more year because we just wanted to be sure he was ready both for kindergarten and hoping it would be to his advantage in later years too.

"A time to uproot ... "
Ecclesiastes 3:2

In spring of 1980, Carlton took a job in central Nebraska, so we left the farm to settle in this new community. We found a church with family activities and made friends.

Academically, Jamie excelled in all subjects in elementary school. Socially, he was well-liked by his peers at church and at school. At home, he and Michael shared a room. Those two played for hours. Building LEGOs, zooming Matchbox cars, and acting out *The Dukes of Hazzard* were among the favorite activities. They fought occasionally, as brothers tend to do.

Jamie was six in 1980 when Holly, our youngest, was born. Acting as a proud big brother, Jamie was helpful to me and gentle with her. Jamie participated in the local wrestling program, Little League Baseball, as well as Awana, a Bible memory club. Our family also enjoyed spending time at the community pool during the summers. Later, we learned Jamie developed an allergy to the chemicals used to treat pools. Back then, it was just summer fun.

Our family went through difficult transitions in 1984-85. We abruptly left Nebraska six weeks prior to the end of the school year. Karen and Tim enrolled Jamie and Michael in Heidi's school in southeast Wyoming for those final six weeks.

"A time to search ..."
Ecclesiastes 3:6

This gave Carlton, Holly and I time to move to the mountains of Colorado, where we lived with my older brother and his wife until we could get settled somewhere on our own. My brother and his wife had four children between them. Due to custody arrangements, the children were in and out during that season, so they had plenty of space to share with us.

I was thankful to them for allowing us a fresh start. The situation was temporary as Carlton was in the application process to work for a major airline in Denver. In the meantime, he had temporary work which lasted a full year until he was hired fulltime by the airlines. By the fall of

1984, Jamie and Michael joined us in the mountains. We enrolled them in the small-town school. The school Jamie attended in the mountains became his absolute favorite. He enjoyed the mountains, the snow, and his friends, and I think he liked the small community too.

"A time to build up ... "
Ecclesiastes 3:3

Thankfully, Carlton landed the airline job. We moved our family to the suburb east of Denver where Jamie lived with us until the fall of 1991. During his middle school years, Jamie continued to excel academically by receiving numerous honors, including taking the ACT in middle school and scoring well on the exam. Schoolwork came easily to him, and Jamie read a lot.

Jamie's love for sports grew year after year. He anticipated and planned for his opportunity to play on a sports team in high school. His favored sport? Football, for sure. He watched it on television. He played it in the streets of our neighborhood.

Socially, Jamie enjoyed many friends, and he was a loyal friend in return. As a fifth-grader, he ran for student body president at his elementary school, and he won. He enjoyed serving his peers and teachers that year.

I think Carlton and I are simple people, but Jamie had big dreams. He wanted to go to the Air Force Academy so he could be a fighter pilot. He knew he would need the full scholarship. Even in his early teens, he was working to make this dream a reality. He researched so he knew exactly what it would take. He worked hard; he was driven. He strategized so he could achieve his goal. Watching him made us very proud parents. We believed if anyone could, Jamie could.

"A time to throw away ... "
Ecclesiastes 3:6

Things began to crumble his freshman year at a local public high school. His long-anticipated joining of the football team, propelled by years of excitement, became a devastating disappointment to him. He never missed a practice. He did not oppose the work or the coaching. Even on two-a-days, he never complained.

Early in the season, Jamie did not have a chance to play in a game. Though noticeably discouraging to him as he came home quiet, he continued to practice his best with focus, drive, and perseverance. Periodically, Carlton watched practices from a distance so as not to disturb coaches or Jamie. He noted Jamie's hard work and recognized Jamie was consistently improving. The coaches never chose to play Jamie during a game. After one game in which Jamie's team won by fifty points, he quietly commented, "I didn't think I would lose the game if they put me in for one minute."

His overall demeanor changed dramatically during that football season of 1989. Historically confident and driven, he was now quiet and withdrawn. Once smiley and affectionate, now sullen and distant. To make matters worse for him, his vision required glasses. At that time, this meant his fighter pilot dream vanished because the Air Force had high stipulations on physical strength, including optimal natural eyesight.

During his middle school years, Jamie grew the back of his hair long (long at our house was shoulder-length). The mullet style challenged our more conservative preferences. This was a point of contention. Jamie defended his long hair. Maybe for him it was a symbol of independence because despite our stated opinions on the matter, he chose not to cut it. We did not require it cut either.

After Jamie started his sophomore year, I knew something was off. He still played some neighborhood ball, but he opted to not go out for the high school football team again. He was reluctant to return to the public school. Early in the school year, he began asking if he could please not go back to the high school. He offered no solid reason, just that he did not want to return. The asking turned into begging, pleading—eventually unleashing pain-chained tears. Although we did try, we never did figure out what was going on that caused him so much distress.

In time, Jamie proposed a solution. He asked if he could return to the school he adored in the mountains. He remained in touch with some friends there. He thought he could be more outgoing in a small town. We did not want to see him go; yet, we wanted him to enjoy his high school experience. Maybe this fresh, more independent start might be wise for him. We approached my brother about the possibility. He and his wife welcomed the idea of Jamie living with them again.

Jamie moved to the mountains in the fall of 1991. He joined the football team. His eagerness dissolved quickly. This time his health dampened his dreams. High altitudes aggravated and enhanced his allergy-induced asthma. Thus, his resulting emergency room runs for breathing treatments stalled his standing on the team.

As weeks progressed, Jamie seemed more unsettled with the situation in my brother's home when we spoke often on the phone. I am grateful my brother and his wife addressed his continued depression by taking him to a counselor periodically. They both worked fulltime. Their house was a full one by this time. My sister-in-law's daughter, her best friend along with another teenage boy were living there. All were the same age and in the same grade. Each had his/her own set of rights and responsibilities. Jamie observed his responsibilities heavier than the others, while his freedoms were less.

"A time to scatter stones and a time to gather them ..."
Ecclesiastes 3:5

After a few discouraging phone calls with Jamie and my brother, I finally told Jamie to pack his bags. On Halloween night 1991, I drove to the mountains to bring him home. By the time I arrived, Jamie changed his mind. He had even refused to pack. I told him I had driven three hours, and I was not going to leave without him. He came back home with me that night.

Again, I have to say how thankful I am that my brother and his wife took Jamie to counseling. This helped me recognize Jamie needed more help than I could offer simply as his mother. When I brought him home, I sought medical advice from our family doctor along with professional counseling for his depression.

During the final six months of his life, at age seventeen, Jamie, a six-foot tall, lanky guy, lost twenty pounds. He had been slender his entire life; however, at this stage I could see him wasting away before my eyes. Once we got home, I realized Jamie was suffering from insomnia. Night after night, he was up with horrible headaches. Light, especially at night, hurt his eyes, so he would remain awake in the dark or turn on a small lamp to write letters.

During some of those sleepless nights, I stood in his doorway. In an annoyed voice, he would say, "What?" Although I was checking on him, I did not want to bother him either. I left him alone most of the time. Oh, how I wish I would have gone into his room and sat on his bed to listen—maybe he would have opened up to me—but I did not.

In November of 1991, after a battery of tests, our family doctor diagnosed Jamie with bipolar disorder. He prescribed Prozac. He hoped the prescription might help.

There were nights when Jamie came to our room. Carlton worked nights, so I was generally there alone. Jamie would come in and sit at the end of our oversized waterbed. He opened up most then. He suggested people did not want him around.

On one occasion, Jamie shared he asked a buddy if he would come to his funeral. The friend answered, "yes." Jamie insisted if the friend did show up, Carlton, Michael, Holly, and I would be the only ones there. I did not realize at the time this was a warning sign. I just thought it was a teen having a hard night.

If he could have only seen the church the day of his funeral. The crowd overflowed into three large rooms. He was loved, so loved. His view of himself and the impact he had on people was so skewed.

During those end-of-the-bed talks, he told me he had experimented with drugs and alcohol when he lived in the mountains. He said he wanted me to hear it from him, not someone else. Although disappointed, I also felt proud of his mature reasoning. The confession seemed to lighten his load some for a while. As far as I was aware, he did not do anything else with substances after he moved home.

His academics still seemed important to him, as his report card from the mountains contained all A's. Socially, Jamie remained absolutely unsure of himself ... increasingly so.

"A time for war and a time for peace ..."
Ecclesiastes 3:8

Parenting teens is not easy. We see what comes easily; we are grateful for that. Maybe we do not celebrate that enough. We also see the struggles, and we want them to overcome those too quickly sometimes.

In eighth grade, Jamie had friends at school, including a close friend. By his sophomore year, Jamie said their friendship was shot, but he did not know why. He and neighbor Chris had also been friends for years. As Jamie's insecurities swelled, he hesitated before contacting his good friends. Routinely, Jamie went outside to see if Chris's car was at home before he would attempt to call him on the telephone. Eventually, he asked Michael to make contacts for him.

In November, we found a small, private Christian high school we could afford. Jamie applied. He even seemed to look forward to it.

One of the school's requirements included hair length restriction. Hair must not exceed the collar, so without complaint, Jamie consented to cutting off his once-prized long hair. Additionally, he went from parting his hair down the middle to parting it down one side. Our firstborn yielded to a fresh look for his fresh start.

His application to the school was accepted. He would begin classes in January 1992. At the time, I sensed he was maturing.

"A time to heal ..."
Ecclesiastes 3:3

In December 1991, Jamie squeezed his wisdom teeth pulling into the busy month. After his surgery, he was much less meticulous about his appearance. He had always looked nice. He commonly chose pants over jeans and collared shirts over more casual tees. He took care of himself. However, that last month his attention to his appearance changed quickly and dramatically. I noticed, but I just thought it was taking him a bit to get over the teeth-pulling.

During the initial shock of his death, such strange thoughts crossed my mind, like if I had I known his death was coming, I would not have scheduled him to undergo such a painful procedure. Then, I think about it ... such a weird thing to think.

I had a counselor for help dealing with some of my own issues, so I reached out to her. I remember feeling confident she would be helpful to Jamie. She explained the confidentiality agreement to us so Jamie and I fully understood. Basically, whatever he shared with her was completely "safe." Upon his death, she did release all the records allowable by law.

According to those records, on Wednesday, January 9, 1992, she asked Jamie if he had ever considered suicide. He replied, "Yes." She continued questioning, "Have you thought of it recently? Do you have a plan on how you would end your life?" He answered, "Yes." She asked him to explain his method of choice. Then she asked him to sign a pact with her that he would agree to not carry out that plan without calling her first. He had agreed. He accepted a special business card he placed in his wallet.

And Jamie was true to his word. The method he chose was not similar to the plan he described.

The last week of Jamie's life was turbulent. On Saturday, exactly one week before it happened, Jamie invited several young people over to the house from church. When they arrived, he awkwardly hid and somewhat anxiously refused to come out of my room.

The next day, Sunday, Jamie came home from church crying, again unreasonably upset. He refused to explain why. He had a trip to Tulsa to see Heidi, Karen, and Tim scheduled for the following weekend. That day, he cancelled the trip to go on the church youth retreat instead. Although I knew Heidi might be a little disappointed, I was encouraged because I thought maybe he needed to spend some time with the Lord on his own in the mountains. I was hopeful for him. Not a bit worried.

On Wednesday, Jamie and I went to his new school to get his schedule lined out for the next two semesters so he could graduate a semester early in December of 1992. Despite everything he had been through, he earned enough credits and quality grade point average to graduate a semester ahead of his peers. I was happy for him. I saw maturity. I supposed college would be a ready change for him, less than a year away.

On Thursday, January 16, Michael, Holly, and I flew to Kansas City to see my parents for the Martin Luther King Jr. holiday weekend. Jamie, talking on the telephone at the time we left the house, motioned an informal head nod. That day started out fine. We ran errands and even went out to lunch. But by early afternoon his mood soured quickly. So when we left, I did not even try to hug him. All I remember him saying was, "I will pick you guys up on Sunday, Mom."

Later that evening, when we had settled into the Kansas City area, I called to say we arrived safely. Jamie answered the house phone; we spoke briefly and ordinarily ... for what would become our last conversation, the last time I would hear his voice.

The next time I would attempt to communicate with him, he would remain silent ... he would not hear my uncontrollable wailing. How desperately I longed to see him, hear him—even the angry, nothing-will-ever-be-right Jamie.

On the evening of January 18, 1992, our board game was interrupted by a phone call, my daddy called Mother and me into the back bedroom. He sat us on his lap and said simply, "Jamie's gone." Mom immediately screamed.

Michael and Holly instinctively came running into the room. A haze of uncontrollable activity and chaotic emotion clouded the room.

I remember Michael pacing up and down the stairs: "Why, Jamie?"

I remember Holly sticking to me like glue.

I remember feeling everything ... and feeling nothing ... and thinking, "This can't be real."

During the following week, scattered memories flooded in no particular order: cuddling up next to my daddy, people offering food for me to eat, crying in the shower.

For quite a while when I attempted to go to bed, I heard his voice, "Mom! Help me! I'm sick, Mom!" I slept so little trying to hear him. I had no appetite; the misery of his absence left me exhausted.

I remember Heidi. She was trying to hold up so strong, so stoic—so unlike her fun-loving, silly self. *Jamie, how could you do this to Heidi?* Watching Heidi alone—such a rare occurrence at family gatherings—she looked lost without Jamie. I remember often wondering where she was in the crowd of people in our home, at the funeral parlor, and at church. On one such time, I went looking for her. I found her huddled up in a corner talking on the telephone to her then boyfriend, now husband Alex. I also remember trying to get into Jamie's room in the middle of one night, only to find Heidi, Michael, and neighbor Chris asleep across the floor.

I wanted friends and family to have access to his room, his stuff, our home to allow everyone to deal as openly as possible with this horrific loss. I remember being surprised when some of our friends showed up from Nebraska to attend his funeral.

I remember not wanting all the people to leave. Their presence helped see and celebrate his life beyond the shadow of the manner of death. Both sets of grandparents stayed longer, which was a comfort. The grandfathers worked together to reorganize Jamie's room. It was a bit disheveled between Jamie being in the process of painting the room along with all the investigating that had gone on during the week leading up to the funeral.

I think it was March or April before we were alone as a family of four instead of five. Although Carlton usually worked nights, the airline granted him a bereavement option to work days for a few months so he could spend more time with the family, which he did do. Neighbor Chris continued to stop by our house daily for months, which was a great comfort to all of us. He was in college the semester Jamie died. Unfortunately, Jamie's death and subsequent grief pulled him out of the rigorous studies, and he did not ever return.

One of my most difficult moments came when everyone left. I was to make a meal for the family; however, when I set the table for four people knowing full well the five of us would never gather around a meal again, I broke down. I lost it completely, to the point I do not even know how or what everyone ate that night.

Looking back, I remember the funeral being such a comforting time. We asked my younger brother to play a song on his trumpet for the service, but he had not brought his instrument. Somehow, someone got him one to play. Despite his own grief, he attempted to play. He emotionally struggled through the whole song, which was meaningful to me. The authenticity illustrated how deeply we feel Jamie's absence. The service included the reading of Jamie's favorite Scripture from Ecclesiastes chapter three.

We chose the uncles to serve as pallbearers, and friends, including Heidi, to be honorary pallbearers. We gave Heidi the option to join the uncles as a pallbearer in actually carrying the casket. After some thought, she told us she did not think she could do it. We understood.

Remembering the people who came to the funeral, from the babies to the elderly, remains a beautiful, refreshing memory for me. Despite the devastating end, Jamie's short, pained life touched so many—young, old, and in between. This pillar memory supports me as I struggled to move forward. Where does a mom find the courage to live well after such a loss like this?

I remember writing thank you notes to the sheriff, the coroner—so many people we never met—but they cared for Jamie's remains. I needed them to know I appreciated what they do. Sometimes my mind would involuntarily envision what he looked like when Roger found him hanging there. I hated it. Agony filled the mom in me while I remembered Roger's describing his red-pooled face—absent of life, yet full of peace. His eyes closed; his hands folded. His fingernails were clean, which we were told indicated he had not had attempted to escape his final decision.

For a while, I wanted to blame the girl he had been interested in at the time of his death. She must have broken his heart. However, with time I let this go. Blame only leads to bitterness. No one thing, circumstance, idea, or person had driven him to this. Jamie made a choice. That choice ended his life. That choice forever changed my life, but I refuse to let bitterness win.

Revolving questions? Yes. Where did I go wrong as a parent? What should I have done differently or better? Why did I not ask more questions? When the answers to these questions never came, parenting Michael and Holly seemed daunting. They needed to know they are loved. Period.

The first year after his death, I did not know how to do normal life again. I did not drive much. After he earned his driver's license, Jamie drove us around. I struggled through birthdays and holidays. I did not want to celebrate Christmas.

Then, in the spring of 1993, Heidi graduated from high school. This milestone heaved the heavy and happy into one occasion. Her life was going on, and she would attend university in the fall. Sincerely proud of her accomplishments, yet we thought we would be doing this with Jamie too. I was overwhelmed with a fresh wave of grief just as I was overjoyed for her. Where would he have gone? What would he have studied? What successes could he have attained?

Michael and Holly seemed to grow up too fast. Before Jamie's death, we had rules. We followed rules. Bed: made daily. Bedtimes: regimented. Metal music: forbidden (although Jamie listened to it anyway). Telephone and television were only allowed with permission. If a show had a swear word, off went the TV.

After Jamie's death, I feared my parenting might be a fault line. I lost the strength to demand and discipline. The rules faded. I became snoopy. Anything under our roof was accessible to me because I realized in going through Jamie's things after his death he left traces of his depression and hopelessness. I had not attempted to know enough of what was going on in his personal world. With Michael and Holly, I did not make the same mistake.

Carlton and I did not blame each other for Jamie's struggle or his death. At least, I do not think we ever did. We knew our marriage was in trouble, as statistics suggests most marriages dissolve after the death of a child. The number goes up if the death was a suicide. We had been married just shy of 20 years when Jamie died. We clung to each other as much as we could. We attended a suicide survivor support group where other families gathered who had a similar loss. The commonality of our stories made it more comfortable to share our grief. Carlton, who normally was quiet, almost silent, felt free to share often. I remember him sharing how difficult it was to focus at work, and others in the group had dealt or were dealing with similar thoughts or feelings. In this group, we felt like we were not the only people on the planet dealing with this horrible, abnormal situation. Slowly, I think learning to relate to others helped us gain a sense of normalcy.

After the first two weeks, our church tried to get us to "get over it." Specifically, it was suggested we no longer talk about it. I could not do that. My first-born son had died ... by his own hand. How do you just get over it? Needless to say, we found a church who welcomed us, even in our grief, and continued to be supportive for years to come. One example, if we got flowers for the church in memory of Jamie, the pastor took time to acknowledge us and Jamie in some way. Simple gestures like that meant so much.

We received sympathy cards daily for over two months. Some people continue to remember Jamie's birthday and/or the anniversary of his death. Pray for the grieving people, pray for comfort, but do not attempt to sum up life to grieving people.

Each stage Heidi goes through begs the question, "Where would Jamie be now?" With the two of them seven weeks apart, we knew we would see them go through so many life experiences together. When Michael was breaking records in Colorado eight-man football, I wondered how Jamie would display his pride as he watched him play? At Holly's high school graduation open house, she came up to me and said, "Mom, any elephants in the room?" I appreciated she had not forgotten her brother. I know he would be so proud of them, yet I cannot express how much I wish he knew how proud we were of him.

Before Jamie's death, I did not know much about suicide or details of death in general. I have learned how much it means to be present for people during times of crisis. Words are not necessary, but physical presence echoes a profound deafening effect on the emptiness that follows loss. I have also spoken at ladies' retreats sharing our family's story of struggle, loss, pain, but also about love.

Sadly, since Jamie's death, one of the families who attended his funeral, the father hung himself a few years later. His death, also tragic, left his wife with three young children. She remains a close friend, and we walk through the rawness of grief from suicide together.

Additionally, I have sought out to serve grieving families. After the Columbine shooting, when the press was highly criticizing the parents, I felt compelled to write to the families. One of the families corresponded with me for a time.

Another young man, who went to the same high school with Michael and Holly, also died by suicide. I contacted his parents periodically to say we still remember. We know it hurts. We still feel it.

Although my pain no longer feels like bleeding, the scar remains tender. Not all my questions have answers, but I do have compassion. Prayer for comfort and compassion is something I practice more as I learned to live without Jamie.

In the years since Jamie left us, one detail still touches me. That is when his name is mentioned. Honoring he existed with the dignity of speaking his name means so much to me. Oh, how I wish I could tell him how much I love him, how much I miss him, how much I believed in him.

He made us proud parents on August 26, 1974. That pride and love did not cease on January 18, 1992. How much I wish he knew this!

> "We were created to live with Him in a garden, and yet we awake every morning in the desert of a fallen world."
> **Michael Card**
> *A Sacred Sorrow*

I will never understand. I really do not try to anymore. I still cry and miss him every day. I wish this world were different, but I do believe Jamie's death made heaven feel more real, a place void of evil, turmoil, and pain, abundant in all that is good. And God is there to wipe away our every tear, forgive our every sin, and redeem all that is lost.

"What do workers gain from their toil? I have seen the burden God has laid on the human race. He has made everything beautiful in its time. He has also set eternity in the human heart; yet no one can fathom what God has done from beginning to end."
Ecclesiastes 3:9-11

Fielding Losses

Michael, Brother

Brief Personal History

Michael was the middle child of his family, the younger brother to Jamie. He was thirteen years old at the time of Jamie's death.

He received his formal education in public schools until high school, then he graduated from a private Christian school. He was an avid, well-decorated high school athlete who played football and rugby on the collegiate level as well. He graduated from John Brown University before going on to earn a medical doctorate at the University of Arkansas Medical School.

He and his wife, Amy, enjoy their four children, serving their church community, medical missions worldwide, and maintaining strong extended family ties. They make their home in Oklahoma.

Reflections on the Interview

Michael's original interview was conducted on November 25, 2006, the last of the family interviews. Although Michael and I walked informally and authentically through the raw experience of losing Jamie, his interview was one that was more difficult for me to conduct and report. When we finally scheduled it, Jamie had been gone for 14 years. Michael was married, in medical school, and Dad to a new little one. The interview took place at my parents' home one semi-quiet evening. We chatted freely, yet time had taken a bit of a toll on the details we were able to mine.

The perspective that follows closes with some updated thoughts and experiences shared by Michael in spring 2020.

Lamp-lighting Perspective

> "The mind looks backward in time till the dim past vanishes, then turns and looks into the future till thought and imagination collapse from exhaustion; and God is at both points, unaffected by either. ... He sees the end and the beginning in one view."
> **A.W. Tozer**
> *The Knowledge of the Holy*

"Michael, we're playin' ball. Let's go!"

I can still hear Jamie calling to me like this many times during our youth. My big brother loved to organize football, basketball, and baseball games with anyone who would play with us, from neighborhood kids to our visiting uncles. At times, his open invitation frustrated me because I did not want just anyone to play. Some of the neighborhood kids were either too mouthy or too dishonest. I hated the trash talk, and I hated the cheating. Jamie, with his love for sports and patience with people, welcomed anyone.

One day as I was unraveling with anger toward one of those undesirable opponents, Jamie pulled me aside. He looked me in the eye, and he said, "Beat him on the field!" That was it. But those words calmed and focused me that day. And I remembered them many additional times through high school football, basketball, and baseball as well as in college football and rugby.

Our dad introduced us to sports, as he enjoyed playing on sports teams, even as an adult. He also enjoyed watching sports on television. We also had uncles on both sides of the family along with our grandfathers who shared our fascination with sports. Dad even took us to Major

League Baseball games all over the country. We flew to Chicago, Kansas City, Minnesota, and Baltimore on more than one occasion simply to watch baseball games.

So many things have happened since those days. I went on through high school, college, and now medical school. With my wife, Amy, and our daughter, I sincerely enjoy my life. And I wish Jamie's story could have continued like a great game. Tensions mount, athletes pressed, wins result, losses come, but perseverance prevails.

When I think of Jamie, I think of my brother whose absence remains noticeable. His overall personality, demeanor, and even dress were more formal than my own, but I remember thinking how he did everything with excellence. He read, and he remembered what he read. He was smart, responsible, and independent. Yet even in his independence, he cared.

When we were in elementary school, I remember Mom made a chore chart for us to track responsibilities around the house. At the end of the week, we could see if we had earned a special activity. One Friday afternoon, I had been working to watch *Star Wars: Return of the Jedi* on television. As I filled in my portion of the chart, I noticed Jamie needed one more X. How could I watch the movie without him? With little hesitation, I marked his box so he could join me.

Late in the evening on January 18, 1992, I was watching Saturday Night Live trying desperately to forget the agonizing moments that had just transpired. Mom, Holly, and I had flown out to Grandpa Ken and Grandma Phyllis's two days prior. Earlier that evening, we enjoyed visiting and playing games with Grandpa Philip and Grandma Ruth, Mom's maternal grandparents who lived in an assisted living community that smelled funny. Holly and I were playing Aggravation with Grandma Phyllis as Grandpa Ken had already retired for the evening. Our game was interrupted when the telephone rang. The caller, an unrecognizable voice, asked to speak with Grandpa. Grandma delivered the phone to the back bedroom. Most people, both family and friends, know that Grandpa lived by "early to bed, early to rise" religiously, so naturally we were curious who was calling so "late."

Grandpa Ken called Grandma Phyllis and Mom to the bedroom. Grandma and Mom burst into wailing—I mean, intense crying mixed with periodic screams like nothing I had ever heard. Who knew the mood would shift so instantly from the carefree game to such unexplained agony? I was drawn to the scene. Something in me needed to know what begged this horrible response. "Did Grandpa Philip or Grandma Ruth just die?"

My conclusion jumping was interrupted by the pelting and piercing streams of "NO!" Finally, I walked back to the room to find out what happened. I grabbed Mom's shoulders so she would look at me.

"What happened?" I mustered. Shockingly, she said, "Jamie hung himself!" By this point, I remember seeing Holly now standing in the doorway. She was crying. Then I realized I, too, was crying uncontrollably.

Sometime before Christmas 1991 when Jamie drove to the mountains to obtain his transcripts, I begged to tag along. Surprisingly, both parents and Jamie granted my request. I felt so mature riding shotgun with my big brother behind the wheel, like a real road-trip. After getting the documents required to transfer to a private Christian school back home, we spent the night with one of his friends. They were nice to me even though they were in high school, and I was still in middle school. We did not do anything but hang out at the house, and we went out to eat. I ordered cheese fries. However, I felt so "cool" just being with Jamie and his friends.

"... OK, so we will do stuff like this again," I thought.

As we were flying home, I kept reviewing the words I heard, "Jamie hung himself." Being both stubborn and literal, I knew they never said he died. So my childish optimism did not allow me to believe he did not survive.

However, his efforts were more thorough than I had hoped. Jamie died on Saturday. We received the news that night. We returned to Denver the following morning. A family friend drove Dad to the airport to pick us up. When we exited the gate and saw Dad's face, I knew Jamie's success was my loss forever. Many blurred thoughts attempted to crowd out this evident reality, but mainly I remember all of us hugging and quietly crying on Dad.

I remember calling my friend Ben to tell him the news. Several times, I tried to say it. "Jamie ..." Then excessive crying. "Jamie ..." More crying. Finally, someone else took the phone and explained to Ben. I simply could not articulate the words.

Sunday night, Heidi, Uncle Tim, and Aunt Karen along with several other family members arrived. Chris, our neighbor and one of Jamie's best friends, was already at the house. Chris, Heidi, and I attacked Jamie's room like robbers. Since we did not take anything, we were probably acting more like private investigators with the intensity of robbers. I am not exactly sure why ... I guess we were looking for some evidence to explain all our unanswered questions.

Somehow, Heidi fell asleep on my lap as I sat on the floor. Our neighbor and I continued our search and talk; however, at some point it became apparent to me I needed to use the restroom. My dilemma was Heidi, who was visibly shaken and exhausted, was sleeping, so I could not move without disturbing her. Oh no ... in the midst of my own circus of body, mind, and spirit, I "broke wind"—embarrassing enough that Chris heard, but even more so when Heidi, in her sleepy state, seemed startled and moved. I was free to go to the restroom. Oh, I remember laughing so hard! Then, I became aware of my own laughing, and I wondered, "Is it okay to laugh at a time like this?"

Jamie loved to laugh. Eventually, I concluded he would have laughed if he would have been there, finding my new gauge for my own humor: "If Jamie would have laughed, I can, too."

That week offered little sleep, maybe a couple hours a night. With people coming and going from the house, I preferred hanging out at our neighbors'. It was quieter and not as crowded.

Beyond the kick-in-the-gut shock, anger was next to well up within me. If I heard one more well-intentioned adult offer me the most annoying lie, "I know how you feel" ... I wanted to respond with utter sarcasm, "Oh, your older brother killed himself, too?"

Yet in the midst of all the emotional chaos, I found comfort in some interesting places. For one, people from church and Dad's work brought loads and loads of food and pop. We stored the soda out in the garage on top of Jamie's Datsun 280Z. We could grab a pop whenever we wanted one; I finished one and grabbed another. I must have drunk an entire case myself. Drinking pop whenever I wanted? That was a right I enjoyed only that week and wouldn't experience again until I went to college.

Memories. Sometimes they surface out of nowhere. Another bizarre memory: One afternoon during the week leading up to the funeral, the youth group came to visit us. As we sat together, one girl began a hyperventilating episode that did not cease until someone took her to the emergency room, where they determined nothing physically was wrong with her. What was this world coming to?

At some point during that week, I remember wanting to find the youth leaders who were on the retreat so they could recount their last memories of Jamie and the situation. I did not want to ask, but I wanted to hear from them.

Looking back, I still cannot believe we spent a whole day at the funeral home. Someone, maybe the funeral director, led Mom, Dad, Holly, and I into the chapel room with an aisle and pews. The casket was positioned at the far end of the aisle. As we walked in, I remember thinking how weird it was I could not see anything until I was standing within arm's-length of the burial box. When I saw the remnants of my brother, I burst into tears. This free-flow of emotion surprised me. Like a Hawaii rainstorm. Came hard and fast; then it was over. Oddly, later that day I stood at the back of the room where we originally entered, and I realized the body was clearly visible from that angle. For whatever reason, I did not allow myself to see him until I could no longer escape.

I could only observe the body for so long until I shifted my focus to the variety of grief displays all around me. My own cynicism crept in. I remember one cousin, mourning in her own way, stood in front of the pews with a sheet of paper which she claimed held the words to Jamie's favorite poem. At the time, I boiled at this proclamation. A harmless, probably sentimental poem ... what triggered such anger within me? There were a few things we, my brother and I, communicated our utter disdain for—like poetry. This seemed totally absurd to everything I knew about my brother.

This cynicism lingered for quite some time. Not knowing how to respond myself, all the random responses seemed foreign and unwelcome. Yet when people reached out to me, not demanding anything from me, I appreciated that more than I really even recognized at the time. My sixth grade teacher came to the funeral. Although slightly awkward, she silently hugged me tightly into her chest. A guy, who I admit I tormented when we played baseball, came to the viewing at the funeral home. He quietly sought me out, and he also hugged me. That day I felt badly for how I had treated him, accepted his forgiveness, and elevated him to the status of friend.

Before the funeral, we gathered in a separate room where the body awaited our final goodbyes. We were given permission to put mementoes into the casket, so I chose an F-14 model airplane and a baseball card. That was it: a couple small items to illustrate all that had been ... left there symbolizing all that would never be again.

Then we were paraded in front of hundreds of people. I hated sitting in the front of the church, but Mom sat next to me. As she gently rubbed my back, I settled into the service. Although overall I felt the service was long, I loved when Mr. Gus sang. He was a retired gentleman who always wore a bowtie, baked cookies, and often sang special music at church. One reason he and Jamie got along so well was their shared love for cooking. Mr. Gus chose a song he knew Jamie liked. Mr. Gus, voice cracking a little, did not sing as well as he normally did. He, too, was choked up. His emotions and efforts touched me.

All the thoughts that bombarded, escaped, and exploded in my mind added to the confusion. Like when we lowered the shirt collar on the body to reveal the deep purple band—no lacerations, beyond a bruise—that stretched from ear to ear. The way they had sewn the lips and applied makeup, I thought, "Man, you look like a sissy! Wait, that is not you. ... Where are you? Will I ever see you again? Will you know me?"

I rode in the first car on the way to the cemetery. As I glanced back down the road that snaked from the church to the highway to the cemetery, I could see more and more cars filing in the train. All these people, all the cars ... to say good-bye to a quiet, smart, young guy. My brother. Amazing, really. I am so glad he was my brother.

The funeral was held on January 23, 1992. It was a Thursday with snow on the ground and sun in the sky. The wind was piercing, but since I huddled in the middle of the burial tent, I felt shielded for a time. Since I was part of the immediate family, I was given a chair. I do not remember anything said at the graveside, but I do remember releasing red and white balloons commemorating Jamie's love for the Nebraska Cornhusker football team.

We returned to the church for a huge buffet meal, which I remember actually being fun. Looking back, I wish I could have been more friendly with more people. I guess it is like my wedding—everyone we know and love is there, but it's difficult to have much of a conversation with them. I remember feeling most comfortable around the more stoic family members. I knew they were there for me, but I also did not feel smothered by them. Randomly, I remember Uncle Brad driven to find answers to the endless questions; Mom wanting to be near Heidi; Heidi, quiet (very out of character for her), but also open to talk; Dad not talking much; and Holly holding Jamie's things.

Our first week alone as a family of four instead of five was the most difficult time for me. The hole in our home resounded in the obvious silence. I began to fill the silence—or drown out Mom's tears—with Jamie's music. I deny ever being a country music fan (although even the author wants to argue with me on this one); however, heavy metal music became my music of choice. A close friend and I made three cassette tapes with various songs that reminded us of Jamie. We called them Jamie Vol. I, Vol. II, and Vol. III. Sometimes, we got together just to listen and remember while attempting to deal with our own pain. Believe it or not, that music and those times served as great comfort to me.

Watching life move on, that was tough, too. I struggled both to concentrate in and care about school. Eventually, I had to drop my eighth grade algebra class because I simply could not keep up with the pace. My academic performance dropped dramatically. My ability to interact with my fellow classmates became questionable at best. I found myself hanging out in my Spanish class, as my teacher welcomed me. I also found myself aimlessly walking around the school alone, completely avoiding classes.

My anger continued to well and seep. I seemed to funnel most of it at my teachers for not being more understanding and sympathetic. The most hateful words I have ever spoken were thrown at my eighth-grade teachers. One teacher actually called my Mom and said, "You know, he should be over this by now. It has been two months now, right?"

Additionally, I would get overly annoyed when people who really did not know Jamie or have a close relationship with him would make comments like, "Oh, this (whatever it may be) reminds me of Jamie." These comments illustrated a widening gap between the image I held of my brother versus that of others.

Mom and Dad attended a support group for family members of suicide. Holly and I went along a few times, but I did not think it was for me. I did appreciate how the group could indeed look me in the eye and say they knew what I was going through. I believed them. I felt sad with them, too. I found comfort looking around the room seeing people making it—six months, a year, even years after the suicide in their family.

The greatest benefit I received from the support group was what it did for Mom and Dad. Seeing them get a handle on this experience passed on hope and peace to Holly and me. Mom still brings Jamie into conversation the most. Holly did for a while. Dad and I delved into the subject several years later on an extended family vacation in south Texas. Discussions are limited now as life has moved ahead. For Holly and me, Jamie has been out of our lives longer than he was in it.

Since Jamie's death, I have settled into a calloused position in regard to death. I am a self-proclaimed "death jerk" because I do not allow my heart to be broken by every death that occurs around the world or even around the corner. People die of old age; accidents happen. I don't care if someone's pet dies. However, I do have a soft spot for sibling deaths and deaths by suicide. In these cases, I guess maybe I empathize. I know I have something to offer as encouragement in those cases.

For a long time in high school, I tried to surround myself with people who knew him. This eliminated awkward explanations. Now, as an adult, living separately from all members of my family of origin, I am asked on rare occasions how many siblings I have. I only mention Holly, not because I am not proud of Jamie, but more to avoid the conversational progression:

"What is your sister doing?"

"She is in California."

"And your brother?"

"Oh, he committed suicide a few years ago."

Instantly, I could lose potential friends as they move on to someone they perceive to be more stable. Seriously, most of my college friends knew of Jamie, but we lived together more closely than my present day medical school colleagues. Amy, my wife, and I met in college. During our friendship prior to dating, she found out, which at times has been an uncomfortable reality for her: "Could Michael ever become suicidal? Yet through all this he has developed a close relationship with the Lord. He is worth it." Amy accepted me beyond the potential risk, maybe recognizing the depth of my growing faith in Jesus. We are committed to serving the Lord together. Our church and family reinforce this commitment.

Through continual studies of apologetics and the human body, I am amazed more and more by our creator. His vast creativity is evident, and his personal transforming work is still ongoing. I am a blessed and grateful man, indeed.

When our daughter was born, we wanted to give her a name that would be uniquely hers while at the same time honoring people who we love, so her middle name honors her maternal grandmother and her first name includes Amy—with a J at the beginning. Yes, the pronunciation is Jamie.

In the winter, on slick streets, I cannot help but remember driving in parking lots to make "donuts" with my big brother. We bumped into many curbs on slick streets. Finally, I can still hear him laughing. ...

Yet life has gone on without Jamie. I wish he would have stayed on the field. I wish he would have listened to his own advice: "Beat 'em on the field."

> *"Arise, shine, for your light has come, and the glory*
> *of the LORD rises upon you. See, darkness covers the earth*
> *and thick darkness is over the peoples, but the LORD*
> *rises upon you and his glory appears over you."*
> **Isaiah 60:1-2**

Updated Perspective, Spring 2020

In the years since the initial interview, I graduated from medical school and completed a residency in emergency medicine. I work as an attending physician in a community hospital for many years. I have had the opportunity to evaluate and treat many suicidal patients during my career. Although I am not proud of it, my attitude is typically negative toward these patients. Whether caused because of anger regarding my own loss or frustration that someone else could be as selfish as my brother and steal his life from us or some other motive, I can't specifically pinpoint.

On one occasion nearly 25 years after Jamie's death, I was taking care of a suicidal patient who had been in the ER for nearly 24 hours. A couple of nurses asked me for some small request to help her feel more comfortable, and, from some unresolved pit inside of me, I snapped and refused as I would not cave to the request of an entirely selfish person and give her a more relaxing stay while in the hospital. I immediately knew I was in the wrong and found myself apologizing to the nurses but realized the effects of my loss continued to influence me even to the present day.

Amy and I now have four children, all of whom have heard about Uncle Jamie. Knowing how much he enjoyed children causes me to lament the lost relationship they could have had with their uncle. The kids are aware that Uncle Jamie died years ago, but to this point only our oldest (Jamy) knows the cause of his death.

> "We do the greatest service to the next generation of Christians by passing on to them undimmed and undiminished the noble concept of God which we received from our Hebrew and Christian fathers of generations past."
> **A.W. Tozer**
> *The Knowledge of the Holy*

Through the years, I have been able to share my loss and path of healing with several friends who have been impacted by the suicide of a friend or family member. To be encouraged by God's Word while seeing a survivor of suicide is a gift anyone can benefit from while they endure such a trial. Certainly, the pain seems insurmountable at first, but, with time, that burden is lifted.

Jamie is not forgotten. He is forever loved. I still miss him. His absence remains evident. It is not his death which dominates my memories of him, but his life and the joy of being his brother.

> "With the goodness of God to desire our highest welfare, the wisdom of God to plan it, and the power of God to achieve it, what do we lack?"
> **A.W. Tozer**
> *The Knowledge of the Holy*

Only Chance to Live

Holly, Sister

Brief Personal History

Holly is the youngest child of three and was only eleven—an elementary school student—when her eldest brother died by suicide.

She describes herself as determined, stubborn, and indecisive. She enjoys crafts, especially scrapbooking. She enjoys sports to a point — with two brothers that was a must, both participation as well as observation.

She graduated as valedictorian of her Christian high school class and went on to graduate from John Brown University in 2003 with a degree in special education. Following graduation, she married Elmer, who served in the United States Marine Corps, with two combat tours in Iraq. The couple served with Youth With A Mission in Chile as well as in the United States.

These days, they live in Texas, where they homeschool children Ana, Asher, and Alister. They are active in their church family, especially in music. If the house is quiet, it is probably because they have each found a good book to get lost in. They love hosting people in their home for homemade Mexican food, good conversation, and laughter over a game. Holly still enjoys crafting when time allows.

How have they chosen to talk with their own children about Jamie and his manner of death? At this point, the children are aware of Uncle Jamie. The family speaks of him naturally and easily. The children know of his passing but not the details of it. That will come in time.

Reflections on the Interview

We conducted this interview on June 9, 1999, at the family home in Aurora, Colorado, during my visit to celebrate Holly's high school graduation.

Holly is the only sister, six years younger than Jamie. This interview took place seven years after Jamie's death in what had been remodeled to become her room—previously Jamie's bedroom. Freshly valedictorian of her class, she was preparing to go to college in the fall. She had thoroughly filled out my initial paperwork with extensive answers, so our conversation flowed easily.

Holly's honest and upbeat demeanor remained steady throughout our interview. She spoke freely. Even at eighteen, she reiterated the hurt is not fun to talk about, but she hoped sharing her experience would comfort others who unfortunately do and will face such loss.

More than two decades since our interview, biographical details have been added to this introduction, and Holly and I revisited the text together. On the whole, the perspective that follows remains that of the eighteen-year-old sister, reflecting on a grief from her past even as she was pivoting toward a bright new chapter.

Lamp-lighting Perspective

"Jamie, I don't like you!"

At the ripe age of eleven years old, I gritted my teeth and stomped away in total disgust and utter annoyance. As Mom, Michael, and I were preparing to go to the airport, I was waiting for Jamie to bring me his Walkman (a popular portable electronic item that played cassette tapes). He told me earlier I could borrow it for the flight to Kansas City; however, he changed his mind at the last minute. How did I feel? Furious! And I stomped away. My last conversation with my seventeen-year-old brother consisted of his smirking refusal and my ballooning anger in response. Maybe an ordinary teen brother and elementary-age sister exchange. Maybe given time and space we would have circled around to forgiving and forgetting in some sort of silly, bantering, sibling embrace.

Before his death, I enjoyed my big brother most of the time. We had our moments as all siblings do, I suppose. Despite our six-year age difference, Jamie made time for me. After he earned his driver's license, he would drive me to the local 7-Eleven for nachos and cherry Slurpees. Sometimes, his best friend (and our neighbor down the street) would join us with his little sister, who was about my age.

As he was only three years older, Michael and I would argue, fight, and nitpick more often, but Jamie would stick up for me. Jamie gifted me as a little sister with a sense of love and protection he chose to extend. After Jamie's death, I have seen Michael choose to gift me as well although his is a bit more embedded in teasing. All that said, I am thankful for both my brothers.

The year or so before Jamie died, I knew he was struggling some. Mainly, this is what I was told. However, his moods grew erratic more often from my own preteen observations.

One evening, he invited several friends over to our house to play games. The days before, during the planning, he made preparations with excitement. I remember him being happy and looking forward to it. However, just moments before the first guest arrived, he retreated to Mom and Dad's bedroom. He remained there the entire evening. Several friends knocked on the door. He refused to come downstairs to join his own party. I did not understand why he planned a party only to hide away for so long. I loved planning events, so when I got older I knew I would go to my parties.

Anyway, I knew he had been so uncomfortable at his large public high school. My parents decided he'd go live with my aunt and uncle temporarily. This required him to move into the mountains several hours away. They even enrolled him in the small-town high school there. As we all went back to school that fall, I remember missing him dearly. His quiet teasing, his football watching, and his general presence left me feeling the silent weight of his absence.

In early November, I remember the thrill when he moved home. Although when Jamie came home, he existed in a cloudy quietness most of the time. I figured he would settle in, and our family would just get back to normal, whatever that might mean. As time passed, I realized I would never really know what "normal" really meant.

When the news of his death shattered through a game of Aggravation, I did not know how to respond. I didn't want to think too much. I didn't know if I felt too much either. I was not angry at him anymore. Like in an instant, I was not angry. Numb, maybe. The following week or two—make that month or more—is pretty much a colorless blur. Bits and pieces in random order haze together a collage of memories, if I can even call it that.

Vividly, I heard Grandma Phyllis screaming hysterically. Immediately, I looked at Michael and thought, "Dad?" Michael and I moved from the kitchen table to the bedroom. Upon our puzzled and concerned arrival, I saw and heard Grandpa Ken quietly presenting the facts. The words weren't registering, but I felt the heaviness. Mom sat slumping and sobbing.

I don't even remember much of what happened next or the flight home. I remember Grandma Phyllis trying to secure her ticket. She told everyone from the counter ladies to those at the gate exactly why we were traveling that day. I remember arriving at Stapleton Airport, Denver's main airport at that time and a place I knew well as my daddy worked there. Though familiar, the whole airport seemed engulfed in a cloud to me. Daddy stood at the end of the gate with family church friend Johnny, a local police officer. Their eyes held sadness I had never seen. Johnny hugged us all, even Daddy. Somehow we ended up in his minivan to go home. Many memories did not stick with me leading up to the funeral. People came, but I don't remember when.

My friend's mom took her daughter and me shopping for a dress. I did not own a black one. I recall commenting as we shopped that black was too morbid for me. I chose a navy blue dress with polka dots and coordinating earrings.

I remember Michael came and went that week so freely. I was not. I wanted to be with Michael, the youth groups, or Jamie's friends. I felt frustrated to be made to stay around the house with all the older people.

I remember being allowed to go over to a home where some of Jamie's friends watched his favorite movie, *Top Gun*. Oddly, I remember joking around and having fun at someone's house, but I don't remember what it was that was fun. I just remember feeling the oddity of the experience in the midst of the heavy confusion and sadness of the week. *Is it okay to have fun at a time like this?* It turned out fun was exactly what we needed in those moments, as Michael and a neighbor friend fell asleep in a chair together, and I drifted to sleep on another friend's lap. And I remember getting sound rest for the first time since Saturday night when the call came.

Cousins arrived from Oklahoma, Texas, Kansas, and Colorado in the days leading to the funeral. People brought snack foods, meals, and other necessities to help serve the family. I remember some guy bringing in cases and cases of soda. He covered the hood of Jamie's Datsun 280Z that sat in the garage. Since we rarely had pop available in our home, I was wowed as it hid his car. Our neighbor brought my favorite: angel food cake. I remember sneaking chunks at a time, but no one really noticed.

The memories, sporadic and few, remain vivid. Seeing the body ushered in the reality of his permanent absence. I immediately recognized Jamie's soul was no longer here. Yes, I saw the bump on his head, the bruising on his neck, and other physical distinctions that didn't really look like him. An obscure combination: interesting, weird, and final ... all at the same time.

Somehow, I knew Jamie was gone. In those moments, without fear or sadness, I faced life without him. I distracted myself by nibbling on the angel food cake I packed into a plastic baggie and hid in my overcoat pocket.

During the few days between his death and funeral, I was given the choice to return to school. I decided to go back to my fifth grade class. Ironically, I won an essay contest. The contest required winners to read aloud at a special school ceremony scheduled a couple days before Jamie's funeral. Under the circumstances, my teacher allowed someone else to read my paper for me. The ceremony concluded in darkness with a slide-show of our various activities set to Rod Stewart's, "Forever Young." A classmate mentioned, "Some girl was singing with us and crying." In the darkness of the assembly and quietness of our youthful celebration, cousin Heidi's tears came.

I think my daddy concealed how much he was hurting, but I do remember looking around during a prayer at church that week. As I scanned all the people, I saw a single tear slide down his face.

Mr. Gus, an elderly gentleman of our church, sang a solo at the funeral. Sadness and hope danced as he sang the song. Following the funeral, of which I remember little, I sat with my Uncle Dave and Aunt Marie (Dad's oldest brother and his wife) at the potluck luncheon provided for us. After a while of sitting and waiting, I remember going to play in the church nursery with a friend.

In the days following his death, my mom cried at anything, happy or sad. She cried. Someone would say his name, and she would cry. If they neglected to mention him, she would cry. Early on, I did not cry very much, and sometimes, I felt bad I did not react more like she had.

During the weeks following the funeral, everything changed. The familiar noises of Jamie around the house silenced. And a new familiarity was emerging: Mom's crying and our quiet.

Dad needed to know where we were all the time; he did not seem as concerned prior to Jamie's passing. It just seemed weird. Despite a house occupied by four living people, the home we once shared had hollowed with the loss of one.

My neighbor friend and I began riding bikes to the cemetery. We pedaled in silence, mostly. We did not have to say a word. We missed Jamie. Nacho runs were never the same, but we continued to make the ceremonial trips in full remembrance of his initiation of the simple tradition. Jamie's best friend quietly initiated these treks. And I am so grateful he did. In time, I, too, would also listen to some of "his" music to remember him.

When I entered high school, I reluctantly began dating. I did not want to replace Jamie in any way. I feared if I shared my heart, friends or potential boyfriends may choose to leave, too. Periodically, I made references to Jamie in conversation with people. If they didn't know, they might ask, "Who is that?" My response was simply, "my brother." People who knew of the situation often commented, "You talk as though he is still here." Feeling I still needed him, I was not willing to let him go, not even in speech.

Of course, most people in my small Christian high school knew my brother Michael because he was an all-around great student athlete who chose to be kind to everyone. They wondered why they did not know Jamie. Was he many years older? Did he attend a different school? I just answered their questions by quickly figuring what his present age would be, saying, "He would have been ..."

Generally, I love to talk about Jamie, but only if people ask. It is often overtly uncomfortable for others, because they do not know how to respond. Yes, my brother died. People do not know how to respond to this in general. Then add the answer to the question of how ... by suicide. Cue awkward, uncomfortable change of subject, weird segue, or walk away. However, I do like to share about Jamie because it's a way to keep his memory present with me. I shared a lot of life with him. My emotional response volleyed between tears in the recognition of his permanent departure and soul-swelling smiles at the warm memories of his gentleness, his kindness, his kidding, and his grin.

When Great-grandpa Philip passed away, my heart literally leapt with deep joy, for I know he joined Jamie in eternity. Some may find this an odd response. Yet I am discovering a rare jewel in grief: a genuine, hope-laced happiness. I face other deaths, and I picture Jamie welcoming each soul home with Jesus. Picturing him with Grandpa comforts me still.

In contrast, I find other people who have not been confronted by the reality of death do not understand the joy I find at such a time. I know it comes from my experience with loss and my hope of eternity. Simply, heaven must to be too amazing to wish Jamie back to the randomness and confusion we still face here on earth.

Facing the extended family reactions has been a challenge. One side handled it more emotionally than I did personally. Too many tears. Too many conversations. The other side has been more inward in response than I can understand. Too few words spoken in acknowledgement of Jamie's existence.

All the while, I am certain they do not understand how I have responded. How can I not be overcome with the grief of his loss? For me, I rest in Jamie's present perspective. His life here is over. His eternal life carries on. Heaven gained him. Yes, his loss in my life is great; however, acknowledging and focusing on his gain shifts my perspective and lightens my sense of loss.

As far as my friends at the time of his death, some quipped, "Holly has changed." They either did not know how or decided it was not worth continuing our friendship. "Duh!" I thought, "My big brother killed himself. People change at times like this!" I released them easily, but with the compounding loss, the wall to my heart grew thicker and taller.

At church, people were nice and concerned initially, but in time they avoided us. Maybe our pain was too obvious. Even so, we received several insensitive comments. People actually said, "It really is time to get over it." In my mind, this was not a stepping stone like a graduation or the end of a grading period. Rather, a huge part of life was gone, and I had to find life again.

Eventually, we changed churches. In the new church, the people seemed more accepting. They asked questions about Jamie even though they did not know him. They did not choose to avoid the subject of his existence, which seemed to mean something to our family.

As time passed, I spent much of my time at home in Jamie's room. Eventually, we knocked out a wall so my room included his room as well. Despite some renovations, Daddy did not want to repaint over the walls Jamie had painted the days prior to his death. I wanted to keep up a shadow box filled with his favorite things, like airplanes, a photo of Seattle at sunset, a model of the USS *Arizona* he assembled, flag flown at Pearl Harbor, a box set of C.S. Lewis' *Chronicles of Narnia*, etc.

Before Jamie's death, Michael and I bickered quite a bit. Commonly, Jamie would step in and stick up for me. However, fairly immediately after Jamie's death, Michael and I responded to our need to grow up, nitpick less, and value each other more. I loved being Mike P.'s little sister in high school, and when he left for college he vowed to stay in touch with me. Even when he moved from Colorado to Arkansas, he kept his promises with consistent phone calls and actual letters. When I decided to study at the same university, Michael was genuinely excited and very welcoming.

For Michael and I, our normal life includes lots of recollections ("Remember when he ...") and speculations ("Jamie would be doing *blank* by this time"). No matter how many years pass, Jamie will always be our older brother whom we still miss dearly. Despite his death, our memories will not erase his deep imprint on our lives.

I remember weeks after Jamie died, someone read and explained the autopsy report to us. At the time, I had very few questions. I reasoned, "His pain has ended. He's in a better place, and that is just how it has to be."

Since Jamie's self-inflicted death, I have known two additional people who died by suicide. First, an acquaintance in our high school, then a close family friend—an adult male who left a wife and children. After the high-schooler died, several students sought out Michael because he had been through a similar unexplainable loss, and he is an approachable guy. I have the desire for people to feel free to come to me as well, although I am not sure I am as approachable.

While others may view these times as horribly uncomfortable, I see it as an opportunity to relate to hurting people in a genuinely empathetic way. Although I did attend some support group meetings with Mom and Dad, I personally did not find it helpful because it was primarily for adults; however, I observed it as a place of significant value for my parents. Daddy actually opened up in those meetings, which he rarely did outside that setting. I am thankful for that.

Personally, I have found comfort listening to "November Rain" and reading Scriptures. The book of Isaiah has been especially encouraging to me. Another source of comfort has come from being with people who are just willing to be present and accepting of silence. I think in tragic situations, people struggle to find the right words to say, but often the gift of quiet presence is all that is necessary. And the power of a simple hug is indescribable at times when words seem so inadequate. Although silent physical affection may seem awkward, especially if one is not too "touchy-feely," honestly the speech of a silent embrace has offered much strength to me.

In my senior English class in high school, my teacher asked me to write on the general subject of suicide. She actually had Jamie in class, too. Most of my research came from my mom's library of books on the matter and news clippings she had collected. Just prior to this project, I passed Jamie in age. Somehow, for all of us younger than him, those dates held a mysterious coming-of-age meaning.

I remember rereading the autopsy report at this stage, and I remember feeling engulfed with anger. Suddenly, my thoughts screamed, "Idiot!

You didn't even live long enough to know if it is worth livin' or dyin'!" Through the process of this assignment, I settled into a kinder disappointment: "Jamie, we could have worked through whatever it was that troubled you. I don't know exactly how, but I know with God's help ..."

One of the most helpful, insightful books I read on the subject was Danielle Steel's *His Bright Light*, which is a nonfiction personal account of her son's battle with bipolar disorder and subsequent suicide.

On April 20, 1999, a local tragedy at Columbine High School became national news. I remember feeling deeply for the families of the two students who did what they did with their pain. No excuse exists for taking a life; however, these families had sons who died by suicide. With the media-hyped focus on the killings, many missed the fact these families had also experienced suicide along with boundless scrutiny. If my memory serves me correctly, one of these two boys only had fifteen people at his funeral. I remember my heart aching for them along with the victims' families. The shame has been multiplied by the response of the media. I felt at the time they'll have so much to overcome. People, strangers, so quick to pass judgment. But these were their sons. Through the sadness this event revived in me, I maintained freedom to remember Jamie with a boldness that these families may not have because of the weighted media coverage.

The example of this event also illustrates the continual confusion of suicide in general. On an individual level, we struggle to understand, comprehend, and reconcile our lives in light of a loved one's chosen death. On a broader level, the response demanded by outsiders seems to require avoiding or judging the subject quickly. This, too, remains a bother to me.

I guess this is a ramification in my life in the time since Jamie's death: I empathize more deeply with others dealing with loss. Dad and Mom were able to send Michael and I to a Christian high school, where Michael excelled both academically and athletically, and I graduated valedictorian of my class. We gained a concrete sense of Christ-centered spirituality we have embraced. Our relationship with the Lord grants us strength of perspective, endurance, forgiveness, and an unexplainable drive to overcome obstacles. I am fairly certain, with my diagnosed learning disabilities (including dyslexia), I would not have been the top of my class without Jamie's sudden death. Somehow, I realized to some extent I only have one chance at this thing called life. I make the best of it I can in the Lord's strength.

Although I was so young—and as time slips by, fewer memories remain—I am thankful I remember Jamie's presence enough to still feel he's missing. For the record, I love my brother. I do wish I would have made the most of my final goodbye.

A Bulwark Never Failing
Karen, Aunt

Brief Personal History

Aunt Karen is both sister to Jamie's mom, Kathy, as well as sister-in-law through her husband, Tim, to Jamie's dad, Carlton. These two sisters married brothers in the early 1970s.

And she is my mom. During the first five years of my and Jamie's lives, our parents lived in the same rural community in southeast Wyoming.

Aunt Karen highly values excellence, order, education, making memories, and creating a welcoming home. Friends of the family enjoy teasing her by finger-printing doors and windows, wondering how quickly she'll notice. Aunt Karen loved Edith Schaeffer's *What is a Family?* She's a keeper of memories and a creator of traditions. She fosters remembering past family legacies while envisioning a huge family reunion in heaven one day.

Aunt Karen chose to stay home with me until I was school age, at which time she began volunteering at the hospital in Cheyenne, Wyoming, where Jamie and I were born and at the school I attended. She worked part time for my dad throughout the years. When we moved to Tulsa, Oklahoma, she again volunteered, this time at my middle school. Eventually, she moved into human resources of a large public school system, where she worked for several years.

She's always been a celebrator of seasons. She's an intentional homemaker, reader of biographies, collector of tea cups, and most detailed-oriented Grammie around.

And honestly, Aunt Karen isn't adequate to describe her relation to Jamie. He was like a son to her, and she like a second mom to him.

Reflections on the Interview

The interviews with both my parents were actually the toughest for me. We had spoken so many, many times about Jamie and his death—that part was actually comfortable. But the articulating of devastation and the growing difficulty with parenting me after … that was difficult.

Many conversations fuse to make up these reflections for which I am profoundly thankful. My mom's desire to comfort as her daughter numbed into a distance … she longed and tried every way she could think to reach in.

I'm so grateful she didn't give up on me. Her answers on the surveys were thorough and easy to discuss. And her enduring commitment to help me realize … I still have a pulse; I'm still breathing.

Thank you is inadequate, Mom.

But we'll start there.

Lamp-lighting Perspective

Remembering back to 1973-74, I'm reminded with gratefulness of the Lord's generosity to our family. Tim and I were married in 1971. Not long after, we were ready to start a family of our own. However, this turned out to be more difficult than either of us imagined.

Tim, second-born of five, and I, second-born of four, both envisioned having a large family one day. I couldn't wait to decorate for the seasons and find ways to celebrate God's goodness every day. Tim went from being the all-star athlete to studying to be a social studies teacher with a physical education emphasis. We looked forward to an active family life.

By late 1973, I wondered if something might be wrong. We longed for children. We had hopes for children. And Tim … well, children loved him. But, not yet.

Our whole family was so excited to hear the news of Kathy's pregnancy. I was overjoyed for them and so grateful that not long after, we announced what would become my only pregnancy. How generous is the Lord! Kathy and I got to walk through these pregnancies together, which included a hot summer.

The wonder of a late summer rain on the plains where I grew up is the scent, the deep gray-blue taking over the vast sky with ever-approaching streaks, and that fresh fragrance. God's rich blessings rained down on our family during the autumn of 1974. When Jamie was born, I'll never forget holding him and loving him instantly like I'd never loved anyone before. Seven weeks later when Heidi arrived, I know Kathy felt the same about her. They looked so much alike. Jamie's face a little rounder. Heidi's more oblong. Jamie's hair grew in faster. Both of them got the family curls. These two kids had the same family history, same grandparents on both sides of the family, same aunts and uncles and cousins, too. But their kinship? So much more.

Those early years, we lived the farm and small-town life together. Daddy farming. Mother canning pickles, apple sauce, and strawberry jam. While Carlton and Kathy lived on the homeplace, we spent quite a bit of time there as well.

During the school year, Tim taught K-12 social studies, physical education, and coached wrestling. So, as remains common in small towns, the school and the church were the hubs of activity outside the farming and ranching demands.

My Swedish ancestors planted the church we attended. Mother sang solos, quartets, and in the choir. She even taught children's Sunday School to be with Heidi and Jamie. Daddy served on the deacon board and often sang in quartets and the choir as well. His soft-spoken mother had been the longest-serving organist for the church for many years.

Huddling around a piano to sing hymns is one of my most cherished childhood memories. Mother made sure our brothers, Kathy and I learned to play the piano. While I don't ever remember not having a television, we lived in such a rural area we only had one channel out of Cheyenne for years. We made time to watch the evening news, but we certainly didn't allow it to steal our time. (Once the technology was more widespread, our rural community still only had three channels available until the early eighties.)

So, yes, working land and all the support tasks to keep a farm going forged a work ethic in me that I didn't realize was that uncommon until I was much older. Work awakened us, and we worked until the sun tucked itself away. Yes, we worked, but we also praised and prayed.

Our morning routine included coffee, circling around a table, and reading the Bible and Our Daily Bread devotional. We prayed for the weather today and missionaries serving in foreign lands. We lifted up others in the community facing hardship. We weren't vaguely talking to the air, but Jesus was (and is) the hearer of our prayers.

On Wednesday evenings, we went into town for prayer meeting. We usually went to town for every athletic home game and commonly we traveled to the away games, too.

We all spent time helping around the farm, though. Whether the intensive hours of harvest or the day-to-day operations, the unspoken expectation was to help out wherever and whenever you can.

Except on Sundays. My dad believed in honoring the Sabbath with worship and rest. My mom prepared a roast with potatoes and carrots so we could feast together around the table after church. We discussed the sermon. For some, this conversation lingered while others of us cleared the table and washed dishes.

Once the dishes were dried and neatly put away, we would grab a pillow and a spot to nap. Sunday afternoons meant nap time for everyone. Some seasons, this might be to the quiet drone of a football game on the television.

Jamie loved football. Even as a young boy, he'd sit through whole games. He wanted to understand every play and penalty. He'd play catch with anyone willing to play.

He also had the most contagious laugh. I loved to hear him laugh. But to see him laugh? Full-body joy. We all loved watching he and Heidi run around the living room. We'd shut off the television just to watch those two toddlers.

Coming from an Italian mother and Swedish dad, people often suggested my olive coloring came from the Italian side. My demeanor, though, was far more stoic. Some of my siblings' personalities were far more emotional and demonstrative than mine.

But Jamie's joy made me smile, too.

Our concept of family was both broader and tighter than may be customary in the USA nowadays. Although Tim and I didn't live on the homeplace, we spent a lot of time there. Jamie and Heidi played outside a lot. They had generous boundaries. They knew not to wander into the fields or bother Grandpa Ken or any other workers around the farm. They had eyes on them but a lot of exploring freedom as well.

> "A family is a formation center for human relationships."
> **Edith Schaeffer**
> *What is a Family?*

We'd often dress Heidi and Jamie in coordinating outfits. I remember their first snowsuits. We bundled them up cozy tight. They loved playing in the drifts. They looked so much alike in the early years. They played so well together. Sure, they'd fight and argue similar to siblings; however, they'd figure out how to get along again. They had their similarities and compatibilities throughout their childhood.

"A family is a blending of people for whom a career of making a shelter in the time of storm is worth a lifetime. ... A family is meant to care for each other and to be a real shelter—from birth to old age."
Edith Schaeffer
What is a Family?

They were like "our" twins, so Jamie really was more like a son than a nephew. We loved them, disciplined them, and taught them collectively. And they looked after each other, too.

Three years after Jamie and Heidi were born, another nephew-who-felt-more-like-a-son was born to Kathy and Carlton. We only had Michael on the farm for a year before Carlton and Kathy moved to central Nebraska. They moved just before Jamie and Heidi started kindergarten.

And everything changed. Although we all did our best to remain close, everything changes when our lives no longer mingle day to day. Oh, how a thunderstorm of tears poured from Heidi when they moved away. We thought that would be the toughest separation these two would learn to endure.

Jamie and Heidi wrote each other letters quite often, especially for their young age. Heidi would get so excited when mail came for her. Their move to central Nebraska expanded all our experiences.

From time to time, we'd drive the six hours to visit and leave Heidi for a few days—and they'd do similarly with Jamie—so we were able to maintain family connections. Mother and I were able to be there with Kathy when Holly was born.

During their elementary school years, Heidi and Jamie both excelled in school. They both enjoyed challenges. Heidi is very competitive in general, but Jamie's work? Near perfect. And he already had a vision for his future. Focused. Serious, indeed.

Actually, Jamie and I shared a dream.

Both my dad and my uncle were pilots. My dad flew "The Hump" (Himalayas) during World War II. And despite being in a small plane crash with my uncle (yes, really ... private plane in a field), I quietly dreamed of getting my pilot's license one day. Jamie, on the other hand, set his sights on the Air Force Academy. In time, he knew exactly which planes he wanted to fly and why. He knew exactly what criteria he needed to fly those planes, including all the rigors of getting into the academy.

His love for aviation only grew when his dad took a job working for a major airline in Denver, Colorado. Part of the benefits package included flying privileges for immediate family members. This meant Carlton and Kathy's kids grew quite accustomed to airline travel. I think they all enjoyed it, but Jamie listened and learned every time he flew. He firmly planned on making his visions of flying planes a reality one day.

Even when we moved to Tulsa, Oklahoma, in 1986, Carlton and Kathy came to visit as often as they could. Jamie commonly visited us on his own as well. He spent a lot of time with us—a lot of time—nearly a month every summer as well as periodic weekends throughout the school years. Even as they aged into their teens, Jamie and Heidi got along very well. He was easy to have around. He was neat and tidy and helpful and not nearly as argumentative as Heidi could be at that age.

I think we all had high hopes for these two, our twins. My own college experience, though limited, stirred delight and intrigue. I hoped this for both Heidi and Jamie as well (and Michael and Holly, too).

Several family members attended John Brown University, where a favorite campus hymn is "A Mighty Fortress." A grand, epic song. No journey is without struggle. Higher education offers opportunities to learn, to wonder, to question, to grow, to share, to solidify our own faith. Sure, there would be days they'd be tested. Yet, I truly thought the sky was the limit for Jamie and Heidi, and I expected he'd be a pilot first.

A mighty fortress is our God, a bulwark never failing;
Our helper he, amid the flood of mortal ills prevailing:
For still our ancient foe doth seek to work us woe;
His craft and pow'r are great, and, armed with cruel hate,
On earth is not his equal.

Did we in our own strength confide, our striving would be losing,
Were not the right man on our side, the Man of God's own choosing:
Dost ask who that may be? Christ Jesus, it is he;
Lord Sabaoth, His Name, from age to age the same,
And he must win the battle.

And though this world, with devils filled, should threaten to undo us,
We will not fear, for God hath willed his truth to triumph through us;
The prince of darkness grim, we tremble not for him;
His rage we can endure, for lo, his doom is sure,
One little word shall fell him.

That word above all earthly pow'rs, no thanks to them, abideth;
The Spirit and the gifts are ours through him who with us sideth;
Let goods and kindred go, this mortal life also;
The body they may kill: God's truth abideth still,
His kingdom is forever.

Martin Luther
"A Mighty Fortress is Our God".

I remember Kathy mentioned Jamie's attitude beginning to sour around his freshman year in high school. He initially attended a larger high school in Colorado. He had to get glasses, which caused a great disappointment because he'd no longer be eligible to fly the planes he'd been planning on for so long as the military standards still disqualified persons with such handicap.

I don't remember noticing anything significant in his demeanor until summer 1991. That summer, he flew from Denver to Tulsa to stay with us a few days before he and Heidi traveled with youth groups to Washington DC for a youth conference called DC '91. I remember him being exceptionally quiet that trip. We'd set up a bed in Tim's study for Jamie, and he seemed to linger there for long portions of the day ... alone.

I remember walking by the study. He was listening to metal music. We didn't allow Heidi to listen to that kind of music, so I asked him to put on his headphones because I didn't want her to hear it.

This has lingered with me for years. I've wondered if he thought I didn't care about him enough to ask him to stop listening to the music—which just seemed full of repetitive negativity—and apply the same standard of protection that I had for Heidi.

I also remember around that same time he seemed to be battling something like depression. He had a battery of medical tests run, and he was quite hopeful they would find an imbalance that could be corrected with medication.

The next time we saw Jamie was Thanksgiving 1991. Again, he flew into Tulsa to road trip with us to my parents, who were living in Leavenworth, Kansas, at the time. He seemed to have a weight on his mind. Extraordinarily quiet, but also somewhat tense. He mentioned he needed to talk to Grandpa and Grandma while he was there.

My energies much of that trip were focused on planning, preparations, clean-up, and helping Mother host all of us. I remember he did talk with Mother and Daddy. I remember him being quite helpful with the Thanksgiving meal. But my favorite memory of that trip came when we drove him to the airport to fly home. Even on the drive to Kansas City, he seemed lighter—less preoccupied or agitated.

When we walked him to the terminal (we could still do that in those days), he checked in and we hugged him and said our goodbyes. As he walked through the corridor, Uncle Tim mooed. (Yes, mooed, a real talent he has. He actually sounds like a cow. We've had herds come across a field to his call.) Jamie turned over his shoulder with the biggest smile, and he laughed.

On the evening of January 18, 1992, as Heidi was out on a date, Tim and I were home watching *Top Gun* (which was Jamie's favorite movie) when the phone rang. We paused the tape in the VCR, and I answered the kitchen phone. It was Daddy (Grandpa Ken). He immediately instructed me to get Tim on the phone. I assumed something had happened to Grandpa Philip.

Details of the initial news escape me now. I remember hearing he'd hung himself, but I didn't remember hearing he'd actually died. I remember lying on the floor of the kitchen crying, in complete disbelief. "It can't be! It just can't be!"

I had to know for sure, so I called Carlton. He was just about to leave his home to drive into the mountains to the camp where Jamie was retreating. Carlton confirmed Jamie was gone.

The next thing I remember: fear! What is this going to do to Heidi? I had worked at a middle school at the time a well-loved eighth grade girl had taken her own life, so I knew the behind-the-scene precautions outlined by mental health professionals and implemented by school counselors. How do we tell her? Her twin is gone. How will she take it? Copy-catting is an unwanted reality. Heidi's close relationship with Jamie would cast her into a shadowed statistic.

I wanted to leave and go find Heidi. I was afraid someone else would tell her before we could get to her—not logical, but among my early thoughts. Tim reminded me that was nearly impossible and suggested we stay home. He called over a couple friends. One lived close by, and she arrived before Heidi did.

As we sat and waited for Heidi to get home and cried, my heart felt torn out of my chest. Memories flashed in mind ... shock sent in silences ... thoughts rushed again.

Tim locked the front door so we'd know when Heidi got home. She was irritated when she first pulled her key from the door knob questioning why we'd locked her out. I guess she realized something was wrong as her eyes darted around the room to each of us.

Tim asked her to sit down several times, but she just kept demanding, "Just tell me!" Eventually, he did. Again, I don't remember all the words, but the pain ... palpable ... as her legs crumbled beneath her. And her sobbing, exclaiming, "I knew it! I knew it! I knew it!"

That night, we knew we needed to get to Colorado as soon as possible. However, we needed sleep. I hoped we would leave before sunrise. I wanted to get to my family as soon as possible, but Heidi wanted to go to church first. Tim decided we'd pack up for the 11-hour road trip, stop in at church, and head out of town directly from there. Tim shared the news with our Sunday School class by saying, "We lost our 'son' last night." This actually was confusing, so we had to explain he was our nephew, etc. The Sunday School class responded generously. They actually collected an offering to help us with the trip.

The drive was long and quiet outside of the reflective music filling the car, a salve to our souls reminding us life is bigger than what we see, dream, battle. We're not alone. When our souls sing, we remember who He is.

Gathering as a family in Colorado felt like a much needed embrace. At the same time, it was all too much to take in at once. I really don't remember a whole lot from that week. I remember Tim and my brother going through Jamie's room looking for answers. I remember wondering if we shouldn't have brought him to Tulsa for an extended stay, all really too late now. I remember Heidi ... alone.

When we went to the viewing, we visited with family and close friends. When our allotted time had expired, I remember actually saying to Kathy, "We can't let him stay here tonight all by himself." Of course, I realized how ridiculous this was to say and wished I hadn't.

The day of the funeral I mainly remember wanting to keep my eyes on Heidi. It was a complicated day, the end of our twins, and I anticipated the impact of this loss on the kids, particularly Michael, Holly, and Heidi.

Upon returning home, I remember gathering resources to try to figure out how we'd navigate this grief with Heidi and Tim. Prior to Jamie's death, I considered myself fairly stoic, generally able to control my emotions. However, tears surprised me, even at work sometimes.

I tried to imagine being in Kathy and Carlton's position, and I just couldn't, just can't imagine what they are enduring. We missed Jamie, everything about him, but his immediate family felt his physical absence. They walked by his room every day, his empty chair at meal time, and his silence flooded their home, forever wounded their family.

Despite others' distant discomfort, I was never ashamed of him, although some people responded like I should have been, or at least should temper the talk about it. (Again, I worked in human resources of a large public school district. Their official policy at the time in reference to anything regarding a suicide was that it should only be spoken of in the presence of a qualified professional/school counselor.)

As Heidi's mom, my personal grief easily sidelined as she was our immediate concern. I remember her silence, general heaviness, like our vibrant Heidi had faded into a haze. I'd asked the school psychologist about her and what we could/should do to help. She indicated looking for normal habit patterns to return. If she's a list-maker, look for those lists.

In mid-February 1992, just a month after Jamie died, Heidi travelled without us to compete with her dance team at a national competition in Orlando, Florida. Certainly not easy to send her, but she'd served as an officer that year. They had been training since the previous June, and she loved that team. When we returned from Colorado, there was no question. She would throw herself into competition mode. This comes naturally to her. This was a physically and socially demanding commitment she took very seriously. We're so grateful for her coach, the team, and the parents that year who loved and looked after her.

That trip worked wonders for Heidi. Not only did they rank fourth in the nation, they debriefed for a day at Disney World's Epcot Center. Evidently, they had a grand time. I remember when we met the team at the airport. Heidi was laughing, and she even seemed to be the center of the fun. The girls, giddy exhausted, celebrated together before heading home.

I felt such relief to see her happy again, but I certainly wasn't prepared for how short-lived it would be. As soon as we walked in the door of our home, the sadness returned. Routine reminded her he was gone.

She could not think clearly. Deep hurt weighed her down and fogged her mind for weeks. Our chisel-focused daughter drifted off into a heavy, quiet place. We worried about her. We missed her. We tried to reach in, not sure if she could even let us in.

We grieved, Tim and I. We prayed. I struggled with people who suggested suicide is the unpardonable sin, and particularly those who suggested this so freely to us in the midst of our fresh grief.

We visited family as often as we could. Gathering together seemed right because we could talk about Jamie and his death with ease. Yet gathering also reminded us he wasn't there. No quiet jokes under his breath. No pleas for football passing in the yard. And no twin.

We watched as our daughter wrestled death, wondering if our feisty, funny girl would win. Heavy, dark times brim and boil in unexpected ways, mixing grief with worries. I may never know all Heidi went through—or Carlton or Kathy or Michael or Holly or other family members. I found great comfort knowing He who comforted me would also comfort and guard with peace our family as we fractured a little in grief.

Tim ... so grateful for him. He loved Jamie so much. Despite our dreams, we were unable to have more children biologically. I mourned this years ago; so did he. But we prioritized and opened our hearts to love nieces, nephews, and foster children more intentionally.

I don't think we ever expected life to be the same, but I certainly didn't know what the new normal would be. I remember someone told me not to feel guilty about my tears: "Those tears just show how much you cared for him and your aching family now." Crying really did help release the pressure within like nothing I'd known before. Grief takes time, and I do think we need others—maybe a very small circle—who will communicate on real levels.

I must also say one of the mysteriously beautiful things that has happened through this is the tight, near sibling-hood Michael and Holly offered to Heidi. Growing up, Jamie and Heidi were the older ones who played together, while Michael and Holly made it into their twin plans sometimes. Heidi, an incessant teaser, drove Holly to tears on too many occasions. However, they lean on each other to this day. This certainly didn't have to turn out like this, a generous gesture to bond those three. Heidi knows she can't replace Jamie, yet I do think she's grateful to be "big sis" to Michael and Holly.

Until the releasing of her writings over 20 years after Jamie's death, Heidi really didn't let us too close to her loss and subsequent mourning. But I've seen her faith grow deep, swell and spill as she loves others. I read her writing, and I know the Lord has done a mighty work.

As a mom, I hear the things she can't say. We all miss him still. This collective journey is something we've all endured, but Heidi uniquely.

We continue to pray our sharing about Jamie—his life and his death— encourages others feeling the drenching ripples of grieving hard losses. Christ first endured the cross before he overcame the grave. Most importantly, we remember "a mighty fortress is our God, a bulwark never failing."

Heaven Draws Near

Tim, Uncle

Brief Personal History

Uncle Tim to Jamie, my dad's name is Timothy Paul Plinsky. He shares with a smile he feels somewhat miscast in these particular biblical archetypes, feeling a bit more like a Caleb (trusts God) or Barnabas (encourager) than Paul or Timothy. His passions include education, agriculture, industry, and cross-cultural opportunities.

He was born and spent his elementary school years in small-town Kansas. Waving fields of grain remain his "yellow brick road," as he loves open spaces. His family moved to Wichita, Kansas, when he was in junior high school.

Tim was popular among his peers and excelled as a multi-sport athlete. He broke and set records. He has an older brother, Dave, and younger brother, Carlton, Jamie's dad. These brothers also have two younger sisters, Lori and Gretchen.

Tim spent two summers in high school working on harvest crews that travelled from Texas to Wyoming to help farmers bring in the harvest in a helpful and timely manner. Tim actually worked for Grandpa Ken. It was on these summer adventures he met Karen.

After high school, Tim had two options: enroll in college or prepare to be drafted into the Vietnam War. He chose college to get the student deferment. Despite his athletic gifting, he turned down Kansas State's offer to run track and followed Karen to her small liberal arts college of choice, John Brown University. He earned a degree in social studies education with a minor in physical education.

Upon graduation, Tim secured a teaching job at Karen's alma mater in Albin, Wyoming, where he taught grades three through twelve for three years. He taught social studies, honing his favorite teaching style utilizing the Socratic method. Additionally, he taught physical education. He served as assistant football coach in the district as well as head wrestling coach in Albin. Several qualified for state under his coaching. During those years, he also managed irrigated farm operations for the family.

In the early 1980s, Tim ventured into business. He served as president of a start-up oil and gas operation. After selling that business, Tim began brokering oil and gas properties, which remains his primary industry to this day.

He's a passionately versatile man. Never fully shaking the teacher and coach's heart, he founded the Jenks America Track Club in the 1990s. He ran for state senate. He's served as elder in his church. He's travelled around the world, including Africa and east Asia as an ambassador for missions and business. He loves the opportunity to share and encourage. Organically sharing the gospel through cross-cultural business opportunities stirs wonder of what heaven will really be like. Can you hear that choir?

Speaking of, Tim is a singer who loves all kinds of musical genres and the history of the music. Hymns remain among his most treasured.

I'm not sure the title of "Uncle Tim" without explanation is adequate to describe his relationship to Jamie. Tim and Karen were not able to conceive more children beyond Heidi, and they both love children. In many ways, Carlton and Kathy's children became like their own.

Uncle Tim loved Jamie like a son. He corrected him, disciplined him, and encouraged him similar to the way he guarded and guided me as his daughter. I think Jamie looked at Uncle Tim as a second father figure.

Reflections on the Interview

Along with my mom, interviewing Dad proved the most difficult, for the same reasons noted on Mom's interview reflections.

My dad's determination to understand and honor Jamie—even in the ultimate sorrow—really became a deeper quest, one illuminating ideas like identity with more clarity and compassion. Who are we? In particular, in the intersection of this finite earth and the eternal home, who are we? This question leads us to Whose we are, who He is.

Dad's eternal perspective grows and grows. His saturation in the Word, his commitment to trust, his perseverance, his hope, and his contagious joy encourage those around him. He asks questions. As he seeks, he finds, and he returns praise and thanksgiving.

Thank you, Dad.

Lamp-lighting Perspective

Right around the time of Jamie's death, Eric Clapton released a song he'd written after the loss of his own son. The song? "Tears in Heaven." My soul didn't question God's sovereignty, yet my emotions resonated with some of the questions posed in that powerful song.

Another powerful song was written by Horatio G. Spafford. He was a businessman who faced devastating loss. First, he lost a son. Then, the Great Chicago Fire of 1871 impaired his enterprise with great loss. When his friend Dwight L. Moody planned an evangelistic campaign to Europe, Mr. Spafford decided he and his family would join him. He sent his wife and four daughters ahead of him with plans to join them in a few days.

After their ship sank, he received this from his wife: "Saved alone." Immediately, he boarded the next available ship to join his wife. While at sea, he penned the world-renowned hymn, "It is Well."

> When peace, like a river, attendeth my way,
> When sorrows like sea billows roll;
> Whatever my lot, thou hast taught me to say,
> It is well, it is well with my soul.

Refrain:
It is well with my soul,
It is well, it is well with my soul.

Though Satan should buffet, though trials should come,
Let this blest assurance control,
That Christ hath regarded my helpless estate,
And hath shed his own blood for my soul. [Refrain]

...My sin, not in part but the whole,
Is nailed to the cross, and I bear it no more,
Praise the Lord, praise the Lord, O my soul! [Refrain]

For me, be it Christ, be it Christ hence to live:
...
No pang shall be mine, for in death as in life
Thou wilt whisper thy peace to my soul. [Refrain]

But, Lord, 'tis for thee, for thy coming we wait,
The sky, not the grave, is our goal;
Oh, trump of the angel! Oh, voice of the Lord!
Blessed hope, blessed rest of my soul! [Refrain]

And Lord, haste the day when the faith shall be sight,
The clouds be rolled back as a scroll;
The trump shall resound, and the Lord shall descend,
Even so, it is well with my soul. [Refrain]

Horatio G. Spafford
"It is Well With My Soul" (1873)

"And Lord, haste the day when the faith shall be sight, the clouds be rolled back as a scroll; the trump shall resound, and the Lord shall descend ..."

What powerful imagery! This is not merely imagination. He's coming back.

Why? To bring his own to the heavenly home. Jamie's life and untimely death rolled back some clouds for me—darkness ... more real.

Inevitably, our beliefs are tested. Shaken. We may even wonder if we might sink under the losses. When we sift through it all, where does my hope land? Why is it a trustworthy foundation? How do I live humbly, honorably every day in the shadow of heaven's hope?

We know the theoretic heaven, the one way up in the sky far, far away. And we're fairly comfortable assuming when older people die they leave here and go there. Bright, shiny, simple, beautiful—right?

But when death steals the young, like Mr. Spafford's family and Eric Clapton's young son—and in our case, Jamie, my seventeen-year-old nephew who was more like a son—when death steals these, heaven draws near.

Yes, Jamie was the firstborn of my younger brother, but he became like a son to me. Likewise with Michael and Holly, his younger siblings. Jamie, a high-energy child, had the most infectious laugh. If he got to laughing, the whole crew around him joined in. We couldn't help it. His joy was contagious.

He and Heidi played and interacted so well together, more like siblings. He irritated her, and she irritated him, but they also could get each other to laugh. One summer, right after we moved to Tulsa and well before caller ID, I remember them prank calling televangelists. Just talking about it, they would both laugh so hard.

Jamie was very smart, organized, and articulate. When he came to visit, he always asked me to play catch with the football. I loved catching up with him casually as we spiraled the ball back and forth.

He was also tender hearted, sensitive, and thoughtful. I always enjoyed talking to Jamie because he had something to say worth hearing. He also had quite the quick wit. While most comments came out quietly, he could make you laugh out loud.

We spent many days together when Carlton's family lived on the farm in Wyoming, but even when they moved, we spent as much time as we could together. If we could work it out, Jamie often travelled with Karen, Heidi, and me. One spring break, Karen and Heidi and I filled our Lincoln Town Car with Kathy, Jamie, and Michael to go visit great-grandparents who wintered in Florida. We drove from southeast Wyoming through Texas and along the Gulf states. Most of the trip, the kids sat in the front seat with me. There was a lot of laughing from those three, as I made up stories for hours.

Years ago, some dear friends of ours gave us a portrait of Jesus laughing. A respectful rendering of him, I think, and accurate, too. Jesus has a sense of humor. I think about the unparalleled joy of heaven, the unending, purest kind.

My initial exposure to suicide actually came years before Jamie's death. One of my closest friends in high school was one of the paramedics called to the scene. One of our high school buddies ... gone, by his own hand. I grieved for both my friends: the one who died and the one who had to live with that scene in his memory.

I think the Lord gives us an imagination to empathize and offer compassion. I remember trying to think what could have been so bad for Jamie to be overcome with hopelessness. His mind must have been utterly distraught, and the burden he felt too much to bear alone.

When the call came about Jamie, suddenly earth's hurt and heaven's hope collided. So real. So intensely personal now. The call that changed everything. Karen and I were in the middle of watching *Top Gun*, one of Jamie's favorite movies, when my father-in-law called to break the news.

Since Heidi wasn't home yet, I remember needing to call my brothers. First, Carlton. He confirmed Jamie's death. I don't remember his exact words. I just remember the firm finality and his heavy, quiet confusion in the midst of rapid-fire decision demands put on a dad—my little brother, in shock.

We didn't really grow up saying we loved one another. Before I got off the phone that night with Carlton, I told my brother I loved him. Always have, just never said it enough.

I also called my older brother, Dave. He's one of the fastest thinkers I know, yet that night he, too, was much more reserved and quieter than normal.

The next thing I remember most? We needed to tell Heidi. Oh how I did not want to tell her. How do you tell your only child the closest she knows to a brother is gone? And gone ... by his own hand?

Heidi's return home that Saturday evening shattered whatever heavy silence lingered. I wanted to protect her, but this was bigger than me. Even as I asked, instructed her to sit down, my soul prayed unfathomable prayers. She immediately slumped to the floor, crying, "I knew it! I knew it! I knew." Too heavy even for a six-foot, three-inch dad to hold up.

We knew we needed to get to Colorado as soon as we could. However, rather than leave immediately in the morning, we opted to go to church. Heidi requested we go. As difficult as it was to go, weighted and raw, I am thankful we went. Our Sunday School sincerely loved on us that day. They listened. They reached out with hugs and words of condolence. They even gifted us with an envelope. They had no idea how needed the cash gift was at that time.

While I had many questions throughout this, God's presence, his grace and generosity ... his hope held me close.

Prayers and encouragement from a body of believers girds our souls with deep roots for daunting times that demand endurance. I cannot deny his provisions poured out among his people, a sovereign, yet profound mystery.

As we drove north that day, I remember a profound sense of questions and indescribable sadness. Where do we go from here?

When we got to Carlton and Kathy's that Sunday evening, I remember questions surged. How exactly did he do it? How was the scene left? What exactly did his room look like before he left? Was there a note? Any evidence offering conclusive answers as to why he did it?

I'm sure not everyone handles this kind of thing the same, but I am thankful Carlton and Kathy allowed us to investigate through Jamie's room well into the night. I remember one of my brothers-in-law going through room contents with me. Heidi, Michael, and one of Jamie's friends also waded through his stuff for several hours ... exhausting.

Jamie had been in the process of painting his room when he left for the weekend, so things were a little disheveled, but minimally so. Overall, his characteristic precision and order remained despite the project. Ultimately, we pieced together enough to somewhat calm the guttural urgency. He left no note to give conclusive answers.

> All the way my Savior leads me;
> What have I to ask beside?
> Can I doubt His tender mercy,
> Who through life has been my Guide?
> Heav'nly peace, divinest comfort,
> Here by faith in Him to dwell!
> For I know, whate'er befall me,
> Jesus doeth all things well;
> For I know, whate'er befall me,
> Jesus doeth all things well.

All the way my Savior leads me,
Cheers each winding path I tread;
Gives me grace for every trial,
Feeds me with the living bread.
Though my weary steps may falter,
And my soul athirst may be,
Gushing from the Rock before me,
Lo! A spring of joy I see;
Gushing from the Rock before me,
Lo! A spring of joy I see.

All the way my Savior leads me
O the fullness of His love!
Perfect rest to me is promised
In my Father's house above.
When my spirit, clothed immortal,
Wings its flight to realms of day
This my song through endless ages:
Jesus led me all the way;
This my song through endless ages:
Jesus led me all the way.

Fanny Crosby
"All The Way My Savior Leads Me" (1875)

Jamie professed Jesus as savior. He'd been baptized just a couple years prior. Baptism is a public profession of personal faith entered into by personal initiative yet witnessed and upheld by a community of Christ followers. What silenced his hope? How could he succumb in those final moments?

> *"All the way my Savior leads me,*
> *Cheers each winding path I tread;*
> *Gives me grace for every trial,*
> *Feeds me with the living bread.*
> *Though my weary steps may falter,*
> *And my soul athirst may be,*
> *Gushing from the Rock before me,*
> *Lo! A spring of joy I see."*

Jamie wrestled darkness for some time. He battled insomnia for some months. He battled bouts of extreme emotion. But his final decision was decisive, tidy, and ordered—consistent with his historical personality. Why?

My own imagination seemed to stew beyond me. Over and over again, I saw him in what I imagined his last moments may have looked like. Neatly packing away his minimal belongings. Removing the strap. Securing its place ... sinking into the pressure ... never to unfold his hands again. Why didn't he just put his hands down? Why didn't he get interrupted? Why couldn't the paramedics save him? Why did he have a copy of *Helter Skelter* with him?

When the family had our time at the funeral home, I remember others commenting about how peaceful he looked. When I looked, I didn't see him. His body, yes, but his soul was not there. Could we uncover any answers in the casket? I had to see his wounds. His body lay so unnaturally still with his collared shirt pulled up to his chin. Longer necks seem to be more common among our genes, so this looked severely off. I didn't expect his body to hold his countenance; yet, I think I hoped for more answers. Pushing back his collar near his ear, the purple ring revealed where life pooled ... and stilled. Where do we go from here?

Jamie introduced me to *Calvin and Hobbes*. Periodically, he would even send clippings from the *Rocky Mountain News*. The brilliant, the simple, the depth—Jamie got it. And I loved that we'd discuss them ... and laugh.

I remember looking through photos of him and suddenly seeing a distance, a sadness, pain in his eyes. Why hadn't I sensed it before? I remember his visit the summer of 1991 before he and Heidi ventured to Washington D.C. He was distant, quiet.

At the funeral, I was asked to introduce the songs as well as be one of his pall bearers. Some people are easily troubled, and everyone knows it. Others, like Jamie, carry burdens alone.

My last memory of Jamie was at the Kansas City airport, Thanksgiving 1991. As he walked away, I made the moo sound of a cow—loud and likely a little embarrassing for a seventeen-year-old nephew. But he turned around, looked at us, and laughed.

I remember his laugh, and all these years that have passed, I still wonder what silenced it.

As a result of Jamie's death, concepts like salvation, sanctification, suicide, hope, and heaven stirred deeper questions about God himself, how he sees humanity, and what heaven is really like. God in his providence brought me to a point of really dealing with eternity on deeper terms. Randy Alcorn's book, *Heaven*, encouraged me deeply as I was considering heaven, the home-place God has prepared for his people. Theologically, I landed with the biblical doctrine known as perseverance of the saints. (See John 6:37-47)

"He sees because he loves, and therefore loves although he sees."
C.S. Lewis
A Grief Observed

Even so, tears overtook me like never before in my life. I traveled from Tulsa to Houston quite a bit back in those days. While driving through a toll both, I remember reaching for my wallet. When I opened it up to pay the toll, I saw Jamie's photo. I held it together long enough to pay the toll, but I had to pull over alongside the road. The tears and emotion came unexpectedly.

> Be still, my soul: the Lord is on thy side.
> Bear patiently the cross of grief or pain.
> Leave to thy God to order and provide;
> In every change, he faithful will remain.
> Be still, my soul...
> Through thorny ways leads to a joyful end.
>
> Be still, my soul: thy God doth undertake
> To guide the future, as he has the past.
> Thy hope, thy confidence let nothing shake;
> All now mysterious shall be bright at last.
> Be still, my soul: the waves and winds still know
> His voice who ruled them while he dwelt below.
>
> Be still, my soul: when dearest friends depart,
> And all is darkened in the vale of tears,
> Then shalt thou better know his love, his heart,
> Who comes to soothe thy sorrow and thy fears.
> Be still, my soul: thy Jesus can repay
> From his own fullness all he takes away.
>
> Be still, my soul: the hour is hastening on
> When we shall be forever with the Lord.
> When disappointment, grief and fear are gone,
> Sorrow forgot, love's purest joys restored.
> Be still, my soul: when change and tears are past
> All safe and blessed we shall meet at last.

> Be still, my soul: begin the song of praise
> On earth, believing, to thy Lord on high;
> Acknowledge him in all thy words and ways,
> ...
> Be still, my soul: the Sun of life divine
> Through passing clouds shall but more brightly shine.
>
> **Katharina von Schlegel**
> "Be Still, My Soul"

The depth of my own grief caught me off guard on several occasions, yet my heart ached deeply for my brother's family—and Heidi. None of us will ever really be the same. Watching Heidi slip into her own silence. Where do we go from here?

Questioning, seeking, wondering about our own identity before the sovereign God in light of Jesus Christ's overcoming death and ultimately God's unveiled identity as well.

Again, often when older people die, we loosely envision pearly gates beyond the clouds; heaven's called them home. But when a young person dies, especially by their own hand, I hear the music, his heart, heaven drawing ever near.

We walk this out for the glory yet to be, yet recognizing that peace, comfort, renewed strength, and joy all come from his grace, his presence, his nearness. We're compelled to respond to him and others, but how? How do we respond to him? Sink into him through his word. As we read and wrestle, we call out to him, listen carefully, offering thanks and praise for his presence and very personal provision of divine comfort. We present our honest emotion and questions, angst, and grief, asking him to enter in and show us elements of his own character. He is trustworthy and true.

"Trust in the LORD with all your heart,
lean not on your own understanding.
n all your ways, acknowledge Him,
and He will direct your path."
Proverbs 3:5-6

When earth's hurt and heaven's hope collide, we grieve, but we grieve hearing the choirs of heaven on the horizon. Trusting him. Leaning into his word, allowing his word to shape our thinking, guide our grieving, and comfort and tune our hearts to sing his praise. His faithfulness extends this life-giving hope to others when they're hurting.

Abide with me; fast falls the eventide;
The darkness deepens; Lord, with me abide.
When other helpers fail and comforts flee,
Help of the helpless, O abide with me.

Swift to its close ebbs out life's little day;
Earth's joys grow dim; its glories pass away;
Change and decay in all around I see;
O thou who changest not, abide with me.

Not a brief glance I beg, a passing word;
But as thou dwell'st with thy disciples, Lord,
Familiar, condescending, patient, free.
Come not to sojourn, but abide with me.

Come not in terrors, as the king of kings,
But kind and good, with healing in thy wings,
Tears for all woes, a heart for every plea:
Come, friend of sinners, and thus bide with me.

Thou on my head in early youth didst smile;
And, though rebellious and perverse meanwhile,
Thou hast not left me, oft as I left Thee,
On to the close, O Lord, abide with me.

I need thy presence every passing hour.
What but thy grace can foil the tempter's power?
Who, like thyself, my guide and stay can be?
Through cloud and sunshine, Lord, abide with me.

I fear no foe, with thee at hand to bless;
…
Where is death's sting? Where, grave, thy victory?
I triumph still, if thou abide with me.

Hold thou thy cross before my closing eyes;
Shine through the gloom and point me to the skies.
Heaven's morning breaks, and earth's vain shadows flee;
In life, in death, O Lord, abide with me.

Henry F. Lyte
"Abide With Me" (1847)

He is faithful to hear our cries, and he answers with himself. We receive, and we remember. Next, we reach out. We pray to be vessels of his love and truth to the hurting around us. Ultimately, his identity is revealing mine in him as well. My confidence is not in me or my ability to figure him out, but rather in the great I AM under whose wings we find refuge … and abide.

Jamie's absence left an unfillable hole in our family. Karen walked closest with me through this. Our prayers for Heidi, Michael, and Holly along with Carlton and Kathy grew deeper. I'm thankful we had each other to walk through it all.

Since Jamie's death, I've experienced the loss of a business colleague to suicide as well as talking through challenges of this kind of grief with others who endure it. I do not shy away from reaching out to those who are facing fresh grief of any kind—broaching conversations, attending funerals—to do whatever I can to be present with the living to honor those who've died. I'll share about Jamie and the lingering pain, but most importantly we remember to share the hope we have in Jesus Christ beyond our present pain ... or Jamie's past pain. He alone redeems, and ultimately he sets all right.

Losses still stir and unearth emotions and questions. Even with the most devastating losses, he grants us memories—of *Calvin and Hobbes* and infectious laughs—churning needs to investigate and imagine through the darkness into his eternal light, illuminating earth's hurt and heaven's hope collide and calm in him. Heaven draws near that we might know our redeemed identity is secure in His.

Those who trust in the LORD are like Mount Zion,
which cannot be shaken but endures forever.
As the mountains surround Jerusalem,
so the LORD surrounds his people both now and forevermore.
Psalm 125:1-2

dawn

"The early morning belongs to the church of the risen Christ. At the break of light it remembers the morning on which death and sin lay prostrate in defeat and new life and salvation were given to mankind."
Dietrich Bonhoeffer
Life Together

A t the time of Jamie's death, our maternal great-grandparents along with our paternal grandmother were still living. Their days paced out slower than their younger years, but their minds kept current with their offspring and their families as best they could, along with national news and local social circles.

They weathered turbulent eras, including World War I, the Dust Bowl, the Great Depression, as well as personal losses. Great-grandma Hazel, quite the classy lady, loved and lost two husbands before Jamie's death. Great-grandpa Phil and Great-grandma Ruth lost a son to an accident on Thanksgiving Day a few years before Jamie's death. (Their marriage formed as fresh immigrants in Chicago's "family-run" south side. Spanning 72 years, their life story is book-worthy, probably even film-worthy.)

Both sets of grandparents were still actively living life in the early 1990s as thriving members of the Greatest Generation. Both grandfathers served in World War II. Grandpa Darrell by sea in the Navy as a Morse code signalman in the Aleutian Islands of Alaska. Grandpa Ken by air as Army Air Corps pilot flying most missions over the Himalayas due to the demands of the day. They all knew family members, local boys, and friends who did not come home from the war.

The grandmothers vividly remembered the Great Depression and made homes for their families frugally. Both earned an income when at least some of their children left home. Grandma Wanda nested her family in Kansas, and Grandma Phyllis nested hers on the plains of Wyoming.

Jamie's younger brother, Michael, was in middle school and only sister, Holly, was in upper elementary. They resided with their parents in the family home. While both our paternal and maternal sides of the family tree had rural roots, by this era we all resided in cities stretching from Colorado to Kansas to Oklahoma to Texas. Aunts, uncles, and lots of cousins rounded out both sides of our family.

Despite our diversity in age, experience, vocation, and life pace, our collective lives stalled suddenly and fractured on January 18, 1992. Time— once common, obvious, predictable—now ticked erratic and illusive.

During the week of funeral preparations, the slow moans tugged and unearthed floods of memories. Pastors and funeral directors set schedules. Family friends delivered meals. Conversations centered around Jamie, mostly his life and potential, and lingering questions of his death. Lulls reminded us he was not even here to shy away from all the attention. Comfort circled among us.

The weight of the days bid us to rest in the night. But only this week. For many yet living, the nightmares begin when bodies are buried.

The dark night that began with Jamie's death provided a contrast to the light of faith that glowed almost effortlessly for years. Sure, I entertained questions of conscience and culture before. But this? Where does death like this fit? Suddenly, faith needed a framework beyond the easy and ordinary. Were the roots secure enough to flourish again?

The shadow of death redefined time. It haunted us survivors with cloaks of confusion, illusions of isolation, cowering amongst a crowd. Sudden and stinging memory pelted. Absence echoed and ached. Echoes and aches. While it all seemed to shroud a permanence, I found myself fighting the murkiness. The lamp-lighting talks with my family provided stepping stones to deal with death with the grace grief requires. I could not concede to living a lesser life just because Jamie did. But where do I go? How fast do I proceed?

As much as I wanted to fast-forward this unimaginable reality, somehow I also received the invitation to savor and to swallow it all in due time, even as a growing quiet swelled inside, ever drawing me to listen, to learn, to linger outside.

> "From the lily and the bird as teachers, let us learn silence, or learn to keep silent."
> **Soren Kierkegaard**
> *The Lily of the Field and The Bird of the Air*

Both in the natural world and the world long since tucked into pages of history books or family scrapbooks drew my seeking soul into stories and order illuminating enduring and overcoming. As reluctant as I felt for a time to open myself up to God again, unmistakable whispers of generations emerged, reminding me of life's fragility and that true fellowship comes in light of who I am in him.

"Silence of the heart is necessary so you can hear God everywhere—in the closing of the door, in the person who needs you, in the birds that sing, in the flowers, in the animals."

Mother Teresa
No Greater Love

Growing up in Wyoming meant long drives across the Great Plains to attend sporting events or even pick up groceries. From time to time, I rode alone with my dad in his pickup with the windows down. His observant eye spotted everything: from a pronghorn herd hidden in a grain field to rain streaking the sky hinting storms moving in. I think he taught me to see, really see, God's creation with childlike wonder.

For quite some time, I suggested my childhood died instantaneously when Jamie did. However, slowly, my senses softened and my lungs expanded again. The gripping tension in my chest weakened. And the darkened vision of what this "after" life would be unfolded, albeit slowly and mysteriously.

He made darkness his canopy around him—the dark
rain clouds of the sky. Out of the brightness of his presence
bolts of lightning blazed forth. The LORD thundered
from heaven; the voice of the Most High resounded.
2 Samuel 22:12-14

In the dead of winter, a dormant season hibernates a hope to come. Willows, once cloaking forts, stand naked and exposed. Snow shrouds the growth underneath. Yet when the cherry blossoms in the spring, when the tulips and daffodils unfurl, when the dawn's rays rise and the songbirds sing, do we hide our heart's recognition of new life?

Little by little, my heart, soul, and mind seemed to swell with greater capacity and gained strength reaching deeper than the grief. Out of the well, fresh awakening and delight saturated my soul.

Because of the LORD's great love we are not consumed, for his compassions never fail. They are new every morning; great is your faithfulness.
Lamentations 3:22-23

While it may sound somewhat vague among these pages, I believe these divine gestures were meant to be personal and tender toward me. How will I respond? Will I look and see? Will I vulnerably receive? In doing so, will I withhold gratefulness?

Withholding gratefulness is an option, but an option that centers around self and actually sucks life out of us. Thanksgiving directed toward the "Immortal, Invisible God Only Wise" helps us see and breathe—breath by breath—the limited earthly life he's granted me to live.

In the vivid wonder of eternity's embrace, do I hide and hoard this fresh nourishment?

Even back in those early days, I felt a compelling pull to chronicle, to feel, to navigate it all fairly raw because others face this crushing loss all alone. I felt too clouded in grief or shame or both. I felt too many unanswered questions to begin speaking at all, too much pride to confide, too much self-protection to comfort another.

Honestly, I have both shared and withdrawn over the years since Jamie's death. The hiding and hoarding are the yielded responses to fears, especially of vulnerability most people stutteringly steer to avoid. It continues to be a delicate dance for me, discerning when to shine solely from the soul and when to speak to others.

> "Artist and saint alike grope in awe to comprehend the incomprehensible disproportion of the glory of God and the humility of the Incarnation: the Master of the Universe, become of the earth, earthy, in order to be one with his creatures so that we may be one with him."
> **Madeleine L'Engle**
> *Walking on Water*

While our earthly breath is temporary and often labored, the breath of life breeches shadows and breathes the delights of eternity into dry bones ... and grieving girls.

Routines resumed. Sun and moon may be the only pattern predictable today. Similar to a first-time mother resuming roles of responsibility after a difficult labor and delivery, energy and emotion simply do not meet demands. In a grief-stricken haze, we went back to school, back to work, back to treading familiar places with familiar people—returning as familiar foreigners, misunderstood.

I longed for the predictable, but I felt bound to cacophony. In *Gift from the Sea*, Anne Morrow Lindbergh once wrote of a particular seashell of interest, "The sunrise shell has the eternal validity of all beautiful and fleeting things." Deep longing for beauty rose from this time, as did a premature anticipation of its demise. Was I locking myself out of my own story by latching onto an unwanted expertise in worst-case scenarios?

> "All the great stories of the world elaborate one of two themes: that all life is an exploration like that of *The Odyssey* or that all life is a battle like that of *The Iliad*. The stories of Odysseus and Achilles are archetypal. Everyone's childhood serves up the raw material that is shaped into the life of mature faith."
> **Eugene H. Peterson**
> *Run With Horses*

In stillness and silence, particularly in the pre-daybreak hours, we make room to listen and to live less alone. As I listened to my family share their grief perspectives, I softened to explore more of my own battle with grief. They loaned me their light until I found mine again.

Individually, we experienced life markers we remember vividly. Maybe we achieved something. Maybe someone else overcame some great obstacle. So we witnessed, we celebrated, and we vowed to remember. Marriages, births, deaths.

Collectively, we had our "before Jamie's death" lives already lived, but now our "after Jamie's death" lives yet to live. Nothing, none of us, would be the same again. Even the elders among our family noted the depth of pain dulled and tarnished the adventure like no other time in their longer lives. Earthly lives dimmed. Some for a long, long time.

Yet our connectivity to eternal life slowly illuminated awareness to the intersection between here and our heavenly home: Jesus Christ, whose redeeming power poured out through obedience endured and overcame the cross on our behalf.

Somehow, we reminded—and still remind—each other to receive breath and to breathe. That breath becomes our offering amidst immediate and even ongoing grief.

> "To be GRATEFUL for an unanswered prayer, to give thanks in a state of interior desolation, to trust in the love of God in the face of the marvels, cruel circumstances, obscenities, and commonplaces of life is to whisper a doxology in the darkness."
> **Brennan Manning**
> *Ruthless Trust*

Sometimes the tear-soaked songs are meant only for his eternal ears. Other times, he moves in morning mercies that we get to share with other souls.

> "If we were to learn again something of the praise and adoration that is due the triune God at the break of day, God the Father and Creator, who has preserved out life through the dark night and wakened us to a new day, God the Son and Saviour, who conquered death and hell for us and dwells in our midst as Victor,

> God the Holy Spirit, who pours the bright gleam of God's Word
> into our hearts at the dawn of day, driving away all darkness and
> sin and teaching us to pray aright."
> **Dietrich Bonhoeffer**
> *Life Together*

The beauty after any death, especially one as complex and confusing as suicide, rises in community. When hearts reach across death's divide, we may not realize it just yet, but we are poised to pray and to circulate Christ-flowing compassion. This often feels daunting at dawn. We still feel the heavy. This circulating pulses courage and hope by pointing out orbiting stars, sharing a strawberry harvest, baking bread, dancing at dusk, and hugging us in close until we can open our eyes, fill our tummies, hear the beat, and find our feet again.

These, indeed, are defining times. A flip side to the raw, real, and honest experience stiffens, shrouds, narrows, and often deceives the depths of our survivor pains. Avoiding the obvious. Numbing. Closing off to how another's life and death affect us. Denial darkens. Subtle, but strong.

I remember the first time I read Habakkuk's prayer (3:17-19): "Though the fig tree does not bud and there are no grapes on the vines, though the olive crop fails and the fields produce no food, though there are no sheep in the pen and no cattle in the stalls; yet I will rejoice in the Lord, I will be joyful in the God my Savior. The Sovereign Lord is my strength; he makes my feet like the feet of a deer. He enables me to tread on the heights."

Holes and hope. How specific he was in his sense of loss, an acceptable offering of honesty that also ushered him and me into a place where stating the absences and echoes of grief mysteriously morph into a posture to receive comfort and provision as only he extends.

I still felt my own heavy grief, but I also received a promise, an expectation of his enabling that will lighten and lift me, too, eventually. My new day can begin in this expectancy. Even before the dew rises and darkness of night dims, our indistinguishable groans can shift and even sing as we squint to see the morning mercies.

> "What joy, when day is dawning and the bird awakens early to the joy of the day; what joy, even though in another key, when the dusk is falling and the bird hastens home to its nest; what joy the long summer day! What joy, when the bird—not merely like a joyful worker who sings at his work, but whose essential work is singing—joyfully begins his song."
> **Soren Kierkegaard**
> *The Lily of the Field and The Bird of the Air*

Carrying grief is often a heavy work, a sharing work, a work my human pride would prefer be perfected behind closed doors. But as we hear the cries, enter the prayers, and raise banners of hope, we encourage and endure a faith building together. We find ourselves in the shadow of the Almighty. In his shadow, I am compelled to remember death. Why? Death reminds me to live beyond the dark night. His radiance casts shadows on the less relevant habits of our before days, and he awakens fresh delights even in the after days.

Those who sow with tears will reap with songs of joy.
Those who go out weeping, carrying seed to sow,
will return with songs of joy, carrying sheaves with them.
Psalm 126:5-6

"In vain you rise early and stay up late, toiling for food to eat—
for he grants sleep to those he loves."
Psalm 127:2

awakening

J ust as Great-grandma Hazel prepared gifts for her family every January—yes, eleven months in advance of Christmas—so too our good God prepares us for grief with gifts from his hand, his mind, his heart. He strengthens. He comforts. And he connects us with a resilience and love like no other.

Receiving Gifts

Our family's heritage was tied to working with the land. We worked hard for a bountiful harvest. Generations on both sides of our families knew the toil well. Short summers and long winters established the contented spirit, diligent work ethic, and rooted faith for endurance.

One aspect of living hope in the wake of suicide is groping with repentance and forgiveness. Both take time, diligence, and honest work. These gifts are received with surrendered soul and without gritting effort.

We were accustomed to long hours and demanding labor, but what about receiving light and grace amidst the grief?

Responding in Repentance

One gift to survivors grieving death by suicide is the jolting check in spirit asking questions like, "Could I have prevented this decision?" or "What did I do to contribute to this?"

I actually welcome the questions that have come over the years. Though we'll never know an answer to the first question, the second one might be worth considering. Did something I said or did contribute to the hopelessness leading to this deadly decision?

No, I am not suggesting we take on shame and guilt that is not ours to bear. I am suggesting, in order for us to maneuver through our new normal, we make space for more personal healing and thriving. In order to do this, I needed to consider and ponder my own sin in light of this relationship and loss. For me, several considerations surfaced over the years. First, I took Jamie—and our kinship—for granted. As a result, I often treated him with too much familiarity and demeaning humor.

> "Repentance, the first word in Christian immigration, sets us on the way to traveling in the light. It is a rejection that is also an acceptance, a leaving that develops into an arriving, a no to the world that is a yes to God."
> **Eugene Peterson**
> *A Long Obedience in the Same Direction*

I cannot tell Jamie I am sorry. I cannot right this wrong. Only the redeeming work of Christ can mysteriously hear my prayers of contrition and extend full forgiveness.

Grandma Phyllis shared, "The questions don't go away completely, but I am not overwhelmed by them." This state of mind is freeing—a subtle freeing that comes as grief runs its course.

Suicide shocks survivors with layers of unanswerable questions. Some may encourage something akin to "chasing a rabbit trail." While some survivors simply will not ask or think to ask as many questions as others, I needed to exhaust several trails. Slowly, this allowed me to let Jamie rest in peace.

Part of this was remembering Grandpa Ken's conversation with him: "I sensed his desire: peaceful resolution." A time comes when each of us in our own way allows him that rest —even amidst our own lingering grief.

Forgiveness extended toward the loved one who took his or her life was an important step for me. Harboring the questions and fears of what self-murder might mean: This can be a stalling point for some, an avoided point by others. I had to walk through forgiving Jamie for his choice. And I asked the Lord to forgive him, too.

From there, I asked myself with Grandpa Darrell, "Am I allowing sorrow to linger too long?" If I am, how do I rise from this depth? How fast can I get up from here?

Before Jamie's death, and even in the early days of grief, I rushed through trials and difficulties to find a solution. Between the conversations with family and life moving on, walking through grief proved to be a long road.

I graduated from college and married my high school sweetheart. These years later, I'm a mom to three nearly all-grown children. We homeschooled them with adventures all over the globe as well as making the most of many ordinary days. We carried full schedules. Gardening. Reading classics. Racing around our yard. Even as I felt a fullness and intensity with my family as their mom and primary education facilitator, the grief gloomed in from time to time. I found the dual mom-teacher role exhausting at times. Yet it was within our academic endeavors and my fears of messing up my own kids that I noticed the meaningful morsels within the disciplines —a mosaic of hopeful threads throughout that allowed me to connect with people, places, and even plants.

With stories, songs, and saints of old, I found flashes and concepts to "mosaically" pray prayers. With Thomas Aquinas, "rend back thy clouds, and show thy light." I found myself looking into the actual sky, by day and night, noticing patterns, shades, weights ... and wonder.

> "One winter's day he saw a tree stripped of its leaves, and considered that sometime afterwards these leaves would appear again, followed by flowers and fruit. He then received a lofty awareness of the providence and power of God which never left him."
> **Brother Lawrence**
> *The Practice of the Presence of God*

Over the 20 years I wrote, researched, and revived this "shadow project," as I called it, I found kindred souls surviving terrifying, horrific, and lonely losses throughout history. Their ingenuity, humility, courage, and driving love continue to speak of the mysterious rest and wrestle of vulnerably that share hope in troubled times.

Each inspiring story strikes hope and courage despite death's dark and dank pursuit. Who doesn't love a good epic hero story? Isn't it gripping to consider all the obstacles overcome? I get all Olympic-glory energized, and I want to tackle the world, to feel the weight of a medal and to sing the National Anthem, but then real loss creeps close enough I nearly lose my ability to move, to think, to fight ... or even breathe.

The Old Testament story of Shadrach, Meshach, and Abednego reminds how heated obedience can be—and also how extraordinarily faith- and community-building at the same time. In Daniel 3:12, we learn they were appointed Jewish leaders in Babylon but refused to bow to King Nebuchadnezzar's golden image. As a result, they faced trial and punishment: a flaming furnace.

Their response under trial?

> *"O Nebuchadnezzar, we have no need to answer you*
> *in this matter. If this be so, our God whom we serve*
> *is able to deliver us from the burning fiery furnace, and*
> *he will deliver us out of your hand, O king. But if not,*
> *be it known to you, O king, that we will not serve your*
> *gods or worship the golden image that you have set up."*
> **Daniel 3:16-18 (ESV)**

How did the trio hold up in the furnace? Truly, they found brilliant, bright hope in the center of devouring circumstances. For a full read, check out Daniel 2:46 to 4:3.

Similarly, Daniel (a distinguished official among officials) faced King Darius' distressed scrutiny as Daniel remained faithful to set petitions before God alone and refused to worship the king. Although the king desired to protect Daniel from the consequence, the edict dictated even the king. In Daniel 6, we read how Daniel's obedience sentenced him to the lion's den.

The next morning, the king rushed to the den. He called out, "O Daniel, servant of the living God, has your God, whom you serve continually, been able to deliver you from the lions?"

Daniel's response to King Darius in Daniel 6:21-22? "O king, live forever! My God sent his angel and shut the lions' mouths, and they have not harmed me, because I was found blameless before him; and also before you, O king, I have done no harm."

Even in a dire den, we see the absence of attack as creative and powerfully uplifting. The king responds so ... kingly. He hands down a decree demanding all:

"... tremble and fear before the God of Daniel, for he is the living God, enduring forever; His kingdom shall never be destroyed, and His dominion shall be to the end. He delivers and rescues; he works signs and wonders in heaven and on earth, He who has saved Daniel from the power of the lions."
Daniel 6:26-27 (ESV)

Until heaven is home, the tensions remain real. The pit pulls. Allegiances align with allies. And opposing sides wield opposing swords—one weak and bent on convincing lies and the other "sharper than a double-edged sword," lifted high, declaring the veracity of God and his steadfast love.

When I feel and face danger, death, and destruction, I'm tempted to try to hold myself up. *"Let me show you how tough I am."* My sons run faster, jump higher. My daughter dances divine-r. My husband lifts more. Yet who out-planks everybody ... um, by minutes?

So I attempt to hold myself up. I want to outwit or run and hide. I'm tempted to think I don't need help or hospitality, even hugs.

However, the truth is blaring and obvious. We're granted a gift to be needed. And to need.

> "Suffering will never be completely absent from our lives. So don't be afraid of suffering. ... Suffering shared with the passion of Christ is a wonderful gift and a sign of love. ... Remember the passion of Christ ends always in the resurrection of Christ. ... Never let anything so fill you with sorrow as to forget the joy of Christ risen."
> **Mother Teresa**
> *No Greater Love*

A song sung at Jamie's funeral included a line referring to how a small spark begins a fire.

Just as society has reason to be cautious about copycat death attempts by suicide, I contend we as survivors have reason to share our stories as a contagious offering of compassion. What if we let others into our tears and fears?

Since I was one of the closest people to Jamie, I suddenly needed people to hold me up like never before in my life. I'm not the greatest at being needy, and I'm horrible at expressing anything when I feel utterly weak, abandoned, and alone.

Yet so many people acted in beautifully simple ways to comfort us along the way. I am deeply grateful for every little thing everyone did to lighten our days. Because of you, we learned grace ... to grieve and live again. Whether we remember every detail or not, I'm fully aware of how your efforts—and especially prayers—held us up for a very long, long time.

Sincere souls grabbed and grappled details around us. We may never know how all the prayers, sacrificial acts of kindness, and words of encouragement buoyed and steady us still. What kind of discomfort and awkward thoughts and feelings did people navigate to extend empathy as acts of obedience and offering?

Hope Comes Humbly, but Decisively

As I think back, I don't remember who sent the biggest flower arrangement to Jamie's funeral. I don't remember my first days back to school. But I remember how songs people wrote—sometimes decades before—became my anthem and heartbeat. I remember going out to the garage at Jamie's home to see mounds of soda and stacks of tissue and feeling the pause ... a weightlessness, not of wanting, but of not needing. I remember vividly fearing falling asleep the night of his death—somehow I just knew he'd invade my dreams—but a dear friend sat silently on the other end of the phone line ... just so I'd know I wasn't alone.

Receiving Rest

Resting in God with fresh vitality—senses on fire for sharing the beauty unearthed in pain and exercised in pleasure, bridging earth and eternity in the everyday.

Gathering glimpses of light and life comes even as we grapple and grieve.

Reaching Out

Have you noticed how vulnerability gives voice—first to connectivity but ultimately to freedom and fresh vitality?

In October 2007, in a dimly lit loft room on a farm in eastern Germany, I stood and addressed suicide—the shadows, the absence, and God's presence. A dear mentor friend who remembered when her German village was liberated by Americans in World War II boldly asked this timid young mom to speak to a loft room of ladies. I shared honestly that, though Jamie's death occurred fifteen years prior, I still wrestled at times with what I thought was the Lord's absence. I knew in my head Jamie was gone. But, sometimes, the gulf of buried grief would rise, and I wondered, "Where are you, God?" This life feels too heavy. But we're not supposed to let anyone know we feel this weak. When the pit seems to be swallowing me, what do I do?

I cried out to him with words from David:

> *He reached down from on high and took hold of me; he drew me out of deep waters. He rescued me from my powerful enemy, from my foes, who were too strong for me. They confronted me in the day of my disaster, but the LORD was my support. He brought me out into a spacious place; he rescued me because he delighted in me.*
> **2 Samuel 22:17-20**

And in that deep place of desperation and despair, he reminded me of a passage in 2 Corinthians 12:9. "My grace is sufficient for you, for my power is made perfect in weakness" is a rooted promise deep in my heart. Even as I shared in what felt like a stumbling manner through my precious interpreter, the honest response of this group of women surprised me. I mourned with some as they shared their loved ones losses to death by suicide, and I listened as some shared they considered taking their own life that very week.

Stunned—and billowing prayers as my heart raced. Several asked me to finish my book, even back then. Their bravery breathed courage into my timid soul. Hurting souls often hide in shadows, some lifting veils from their own losses while others contemplate their own demise.

Yet God intends to illuminate himself by displaying unmistakable divine strength in his people who are impeccably weak apart from Him. "Rejoice with those who rejoice; mourn with those who mourn" (Romans 12:15).

The prayers and prodding of my dear German friends kindled a fire within me. Although darkness, fragments, and fears may taunt us for a lifetime, we can live in the light. When we seek, we find. I whispered prayers to the Lord, asking him that one day I may return with the book for them.

In January 2007, on the 15th anniversary of Jamie's death, I planned a writing retreat at the very camp where he chose to take his last breath. My husband and I drove through blinding, icy conditions through the panhandle of Oklahoma to the Rockies. When we arrived at the camp, we found three and a half feet of snow huddled down several rustic cabins. We spent a week there. I wrote nearly 12 hours every day. I remember the breathless exhilaration as we'd venture out to the dining hall a couple times a day. I've never known such corralled emotion as well as expedited clarity. And the deer! They appeared poised and queued outside our window, the snow drifts up to their chests. They'd bound and still, and their stares seemed to endorse my efforts, too.

This camp welcomed me despite the shadow they endured due to Jamie's decision. And my dear husband? His patience that week was astonishing, really. There was not much to do around the camp when another blizzard dropped another foot of snow while we were there. Such grace.

Fresh Faithfulness

When we step out of our shadows (trembling as our knees may be) and speak out of those deep places, we can delight and ignite hope. Despite death's haunting, hope relentlessly delights, still. And as we release shards and beams of our story here, I pray you come to know and delight in hope's tender, yet mighty, eternal embrace.

We returned to Germany in winter 2015. I joined my husband on a business trip to Berlin. While we were there, I ventured out some; however, I mainly used it as a writing retreat.

During a sweet reunion, a dear friend in Germany asked me if I had a copy of the book for her. When I looked into her longing, then deeply disappointed eyes, my excuses cramped up in my throat. That hit me. She's been waiting since 2007 to hold a copy of our story. I had locked it away with insecurities. I am sorry this took me way too long.

Again, how could I keep this offering buried? Doubts. Fears. Pride. Well, my writer's hand returned on that brilliant trip to Berlin. The thoughts: uncontainable. The energy and clarity: undeniable. So much so that before I left Germany, I strategized and gave myself some timelines.

There may have been an acceptable amount of incubating this project needed. However, long since, I seized control, tied it up tight, and tucked it far away. A turning away is necessary. A turning away from the hindrances and a turning toward the One who lifts our gaze and delights to shine his glory out of dark spaces.

My heart breaks for the mourning and hurting among us. Yet, we help each other look around and see the pulsing joys. Beyond regrets, ice storms, hiding ... we find freedom in confession. Like the deer in the snow, we catch our breath, praise him even in the hardness, and bound higher still.

Even so, we relate.

> *The disciples went and woke him, saying, "Master, Master,*
> *we're going to drown!" He got up and rebuked the wind*
> *and the raging waters; the storm subsided, and all was calm.*
> *"Where is your faith?" he asked his disciples. In fear and*
> *amazement they asked one another, "Who is this?*
> *He commands even the winds and the water, and they obey him."*
> **Luke 8:24-25**

He remains both mighty and tender. He's true to his all-sufficiency, and he's kind to display his character among us in ways that draw us to love him with all our heart, all our soul, all our mind, and all our strength. We watch in wonder and press in to partner with him as he chooses to pour out love through us to others.

Psalm 42

As the deer pants for streams of water,
 so my soul pants for you, my God.
My soul thirsts for God, for the living God.
 When can I go and meet with God?
My tears have been my food
 day and night,
while people say to me all day long,
 "Where is your God?"
These things I remember
 as I pour out my soul:
how I used to go to the house of God
 under the protection of the Mighty One[d]
with shouts of joy and praise
 among the festive throng.

Why, my soul, are you downcast?
 Why so disturbed within me?
Put your hope in God,
 for I will yet praise him,
 my Savior and my God.
My soul is downcast within me;
 therefore I will remember you
from the land of the Jordan,
 the heights of Hermon—from Mount Mizar.
Deep calls to deep
 in the roar of your waterfalls;
all your waves and breakers
 have swept over me.
By day the LORD directs his love,
 at night his song is with me—
 a prayer to the God of my life.
I say to God my Rock,
 "Why have you forgotten me?
Why must I go about mourning,
 oppressed by the enemy?"
My bones suffer mortal agony
 as my foes taunt me,
saying to me all day long,
 "Where is your God?"
Why, my soul, are you downcast?
 Why so disturbed within me?
Put your hope in God,
 for I will yet praise him,
 my Savior and my God.

The beauty? We may wrestle still, some days more than others. But we now know we are awake—and not alone—encouraging each other in this contagion of compassion propelled by the power of the nearness of the Creator and the embrace of the Great Comforter.

"Blessed are all who fear the LORD, who walk in obedience to him. May the LORD bless you from Zion; may you see the prosperity of Jerusalem all the days of your life."
Psalm 128:1, 5

"But the LORD is righteous ..."
Psalm 129:4a

*"Put your hope in the LORD, for with the LORD
is unfailing love and with him is full redemption."*
Psalm 130:7

long shadows

Uncle Tim's comments at Jamie's funeral

As I was sitting here, I was thinking. You know if we had a meeting like this—especially you guys who had Jamie in church—you know good and well that if there was a meeting like this he would be back with the kids helping to babysit your kids right now. You know without a doubt that's where he'd be. And he would also be really reluctant to let them go as you left.

... We know—we don't guess, we don't hope (hope in an English term)—but we know where Jamie's at.

In fact, I loved what Brad said yesterday. When I asked him how did Jamie look, he said, "Well that isn't ... that isn't Jamie ... though that may have been what he was housed in on this earth in the seventeen years that he spent here, but that's not him." And he said, "I never felt like that was him. He is gone. " He is, as the song says, in the very presence of our Savior. That's where he's at. And that is a great comfort even though we wrestle with the pain of his loss.

... It's amazing to me the lives this guy touched. The people in Tulsa where we live, the lives that he touched, and the pain that the people that we know down there who wish that they could be here. Jamie spent a lot of time with us down there. It's just amazing to me the lives that he touched.

... I'm reminded of when Dawson Trotman (founder of the Navigators) died. He was on a lake; he was in a boat on the lake. The boat lurched for some reason, and two girls who couldn't swim very well fell out. He got in the water and splashed around and got these two girls out. And just as the guy went down to reach Dawson Trotman, he sank down. ... He drowned. ... He died. At his funeral, Billy Graham preached the service. And I thought the interesting thing is that there were reporters there from *TIME* and a bunch of places, but there was a caption that reflected his life, and I thought what a tribute for all of us to have said of our lives. The caption read: "Always holding somebody up."

And I think that really reflects, and it reflected—past tense, now—what Jamie's life was. And even though there were times obviously he didn't understand how much we wanted to hold him up, but he really did have a tremendous desire to hold other people up.

—Tim Plinsky, January 1991

Do nothing from selfish ambition or conceit,
but in humility count others more significant than yourselves.
Philippians 2:3 (ESV)

s we journey the epic endeavors of ordinary life, including the pangs of grief and scars left as survivors of suicide, we know souls who so seamlessly call out hope and happiness in the bleakest moments. When they rally, people around them rise above disheartening circumstances and join a contagion—if only by a breath—of inspiration and ride on.

We know people who journey alongside us when we are fun—and when we are frozen ... with fears, in grief. They're patient and tender. And they risk upsetting us by calling us back to life again. Sometimes, it takes some remembering, some savoring, some hoping. *"Holding somebody up."*

Who rallied around you in your darkest night, your deepest loss?

Since Jamie and I were born seven weeks apart, I became the family mile-marker of where Jamie's life might be today. No, this hasn't been easy. Sometimes, when I was newly married and a young mom I felt like I was failing to some imaginary, mostly unspoken standard of what Jamie's life might have been like. The truth: That use of my imagination was not helpful.

Because I was one of the closest people to Jamie, I felt the honor and obligation to "hold somebody up." I took over as a big sister to Michael and Holly. Jamie loved them both, so I'd try to love them and look out for them more. (Being an only child myself, I now know I had no idea what it means to be a sibling, but I gave it the ol' heave-ho.) I sent Mother's Day and Father's Day greetings to Jamie's parents as well as my own. Even his best friend and I became fairly close through periodic letters and phone calls. I thought I needed to be strong enough (or at least okay) for them. Overall, I think these were genuine and proper responses for a time.

However, I suddenly needed people to hold me up. I'm not the greatest at being needy, and I'm horrible at expressing anything under heavy emotional weights. Honestly, I hid for a long time. As my mom (Jamie's Aunt Karen) shared, "Until twenty years passed, Heidi really didn't let us too close to her loss and subsequent mourning. But I've seen her faith grow deep, swell and spill as she loves others. I read her writing, and I know the Lord's done a mighty work. ... I hear the things she can't say."

People and prayer. Reaching out and reaching in ... offer healing balm, even when it takes time for the hurt to heal.

> "Prayer enlarges the heart until it is capable of containing God's gift of Himself. Ask and seek and your heart will grow big enough to receive Him and keep Him as your own. ... Let us pray on behalf of those who do not [yet] pray."
>
> **Mother Teresa**
> *No Greater Love*

After the shock dissolved, the new day-to-day was marked by Jamie's absence and the prevailing silence of so many who don't know how to mourn formally or how long real grief lasts. I remember the few souls who spoke his name, dared to ask how I was doing, and shared songs, quotes, questions, etc. Simple gestures? Grand stepping stones for grieving hearts. *Someone is always holding us up.*

How much it means—even to this day—how much we feel upheld to know people remember Jamie, our loss, our pain, and speak life into healing spaces of our hearts. Yes, scars remain. However, sincere souls grabbed and grappled details around us. We may never know how all the prayers, sacrificial acts of kindness, and words of encouragement buoyed and steady us still.

Even as the prayers are extended toward us, we learn we, too, get to extend prayer on another's behalf as well— even in our moments of weariness and weakness. As Mother Teresa wrote, "Prayer is as necessary as the air, as the blood in our body, as anything, to keep us alive to the grace of God. ... We should make every effort to walk in the presence of God, to see God in all the persons we meet, to live our prayer throughout the day."

Some shadows, like death and absence, are shocking and obvious. Others sneak in more subtly and attempt to sabotage and steal from our living bright lives. Haunting feelings of shame for some, rejection for others, even betrayal can slowly slink us into quiet corners. It's a cycle of unhealthy thoughts and regurgitating fears.

Some beams brew, so we first see contrast, but then we step into light. Learning to lean into Scriptures and prayer casts light on darkness and helped me cast my burdens and my deep empathies for others upon the able shoulders of the Lord. If the words would not come, I scoured Scriptures for past prayers to pray upon my present struggles or of those I love.

Remembering to remember remains one of my stepping stones into prayer. What exactly do I remember? Often, just out of pure energy, I remember pain. I remember God's character—his goodness, all-sufficiency, faithfulness, tenderness, and his daring delight in us. I call out to him, and I ask him to remind me who I am in him. I ask him how he'd like me to love and serve people I see going through hard times.

Out of the depths I cry to you, LORD; Lord, hear my voice.
Let your ears be attentive to my cry for mercy. ... I wait for the
LORD, my whole being waits, and in his word I put my hope.
I wait for the Lord more than watchmen wait for the morning,
more than watchmen wait for the morning.
Psalm 130:1-2, 5-6

And I wait upon him. As I wait, I sometimes remain still and silent. Other times, I offer specific ideas of kindness and ask for him to help me to reach out. The truth is my heart still races, my face still flushes. I get nervous to respond to hurting friends. But in remembering who I am in him, recalling his character displayed in creation, carried out in the Scriptures, fulfilled in Christ, I am poised. We are poised to be jars of clay for the power of the Spirit to pour out beauty, goodness, and truth—even amidst shadows.

David sang to the LORD the words of this song when the LORD
delivered him from the hand of all his enemies and from the hand
of Saul. He said: "The LORD is my rock, my fortress and my
deliverer; my God is my rock, in whom I take refuge, my shield
and the horn of my salvation. He is my stronghold, my refuge and
my savior—from violent people you save me. I called to the LORD,
who is worthy of praise, and have been saved from my enemies."
2 Samuel 22:1-4

A staggering steadiness can arise even as a sinking exhausts.

... exhilarating fears, depleting losses ... sorrow ... stillness ... aching
sustaining ... yearning ... past ... savors shrink ... then slumps ...
sulks and strives ... to sip a savor ... only to sink ... {a guttural gasp}
Then ... sings ...
heart songs erratic with lament,
joy, angst,
release, rest, tension, and time ...
and then ... stands again.

But sometimes, we sabotage the standing. Anger, impatience, arrogance. Even simple self-protection can become an excuse—or even an idol—to run from compassion. Rather than wrestling through, we choose to starve our souls by perpetually hiding, cowering from the very One—bent, bruised and broken—who can preserve and nourish us with steadfast love. We refuse him even as he offers to sustain us. We refuse those he sends with a message of conviction, correction, and comfort.

Consider Jonah. When God, out of his holy compassion for a city under sin's siege, called Jonah to go to Nineveh, he recoiled and fled to Tarshish to avoid obedience. God "hurled a great wind upon the sea ... so that the ship threatened to break up" (Jonah 1:4). The turbulent crew eventually toss Jonah overboard. You know, the big fish swallowed him. For three dark, dank, and stinky days, Jonah barreled around the sea. Then Jonah prayed. (His prayer is recorded in Jonah 2. A worthy read, indeed. However, I'm just going to share a few verses here.)

"When my life was fainting away, I remembered the LORD,
and my prayer came to you, into your holy temple. Those
who pay regard to vain idols forsake their hope of steadfast love.
But I with voice of thanksgiving will sacrifice to you;
what I have vowed I will pay. Salvation belongs to the LORD."
Jonah 2:7-10 (ESV)

The fish obediently spewed Jonah out on dry ground where again God called Jonah to go to Nineveh to deliver a daunting, damning message to this city. The message: In a matter of 40 days, the city would be destroyed. The city believed the message. The people responded. Immediately, the people called for fasting and mourning among themselves. Their king, in utter devastation of this news, decreed a fast and pleaded to God to spare them: "Let everyone turn from his evil way and from the violence that is in his hands. Who knows? God may turn and relent and turn from his fierce anger, so that we may not perish" (Jonah 3:8).

God's response? In his great mercy, God saw their repentance and relented of the disaster doomed upon them by their own consequence (Jonah 3:10). He's always holding somebody up.

Interestingly, Jonah's response this time: anger at the Lord's compassion and consistent character: "O LORD, is not this what I said when I was yet in my country? This is why I made haste to flee to Tarshish; for I knew that you are a gracious God and merciful, slow to anger and abounding in steadfast love, and relenting from disaster. Therefore now, O LORD, please take my life from me, for it is better for me to die than to live" (Jonah 4:2-3, ESV).

Again, Jonah pulls away to pout. Even so, God grew a plant to shade Jonah—"to save him from his discomfort" (Jonah 4:6). Jonah responds with gladness. But in the morning, God sends a worm to devour the plant. And again, Jonah asks to die.

The Lord's response, "You pity the plant, for which you did not labor, nor did you make it grow, which came into being in the night and perished in a night. And should not I pity Nineveh, that great city, in which there are more than 120,000 persons who do not know their right hand from their left?" (Jonah 4:10-11).

How many countless times has my heart echoed Jonah's first prayer of submission followed by God's response—resounding power and presence—only for me to anticipate impending disaster and his grace?

"Let each of you look not only to his own interest, but also to the interests of others. Have this mind among yourselves, which is yours in Christ Jesus, who, though He was in the form of God, did not count equality with God a thing to be grasped, but emptied Himself, by taking the form of a servant, being born in the likeness of men. And being found in human form, He humbled Himself by becoming obedient to the point of death, even death on a cross. Therefore God as highly exalted Him and bestowed an Him the Name that is above every name, so that at the Name of Jesus every knee should bow, in heaven and on earth and under the earth, and every tongue confess that Jesus Christ is Lord, to the glory of God the Father."
Philippians 2:4-11 (ESV)

Recognizing a cosmic conflict wages on, we rejoice in the Lord—Jesus is indeed the Christ. And he calls out his people, citizens of heaven, to pulse with an ever-increasing awareness that:

Christ's resurrection reaches out to others ... authentically, naturally ...
humbly, sacrificially ...
Yet Endures, Overcomes, Redeems.
Reconciles, Renews, Refreshes.
Gathers. Relaxes. Relishes. Savors.
Shares. And Remembers.

How do we respond? If we accept his grace gift, we receive the power and purity therein. And we're his extensions of hope and joy and peace to those around us, not because we can sing the loudest, smile the brightest, or even stand the straightest. No, even in our own brokenness, he is our living hope—not to hide or hoard, but to share.

Our righteousness is his transforming work in and among us. He grants us historic examples in his word of soul struggles we'll face, but he also grants us responsive examples who relate to our struggles to fully trust him when waves chide and crash all around. Our lives beat, moan, and sing our responses to him. A fellowship in suffering ... and in song.

Epic endurance, witnesses waving us home, we may never know how all the prayers, sacrificial acts, and encouragement from saints of old buoyed and steady us still.

What if, in our weakness and confusion, we kneel down? I mean really kneel down and pray. We're reminded our citizenship ranks on a higher plane than where we find ourselves, yet we can't pretend it all away. We can't conquer all the wrong, and we can't even right enough wrongs to feel right again.

Navigating the now ... that's the tough space. But we must remember we aren't alone, and we must remind each other we aren't alone. We're being held up, and we're holding up. We join Paul's prayer:

"And it is my prayer that your love may abound more and more,
with knowledge and all discernment, so that you may approve

what is excellent, and so be pure and blameless for the day of
Christ, filled with the fruit of righteousness that comes through
Jesus Christ, to the glory and praise of God."
Philippians 1:9-11 (ESV)

First, Matthew 14:22-33 recounts the mysterious majesty of Jesus Christ when he walked on the water—perilous, swirling-waves-and-winds kind of water. At first, even his disciples feared him because they thought he was a ghost. Once they knew it was him, Peter played bold and asked to be invited to join him on the sea as the storm raged on. Peter got out of the boat. He actually walked on water, too. Then, he saw the wind, he began to sink, and he cried out "Lord, save me!"

Jesus immediately reached out his hand and took hold of him
saying to him, "O you of little faith, why did you doubt?" And
when they got into the boat, the wind ceased. And those in the boat
worshiped him, saying, "Truly you are the Son of God."
Matthew 14:31-33 (ESV)

We see Jesus faithfully save Peter, join the others in the boat, calm the storm. And they respond how? They worship him by declaring *who he is.*

Next, John 11 recounts the story of Lazarus' death and Jesus' response. Jesus speaks of being the resurrection and the life in verses 17-27. This he speaks to Martha even after Lazarus has been buried for four days. Jesus asks if she believes him, and she responds, "Yes, Lord; I believe that you are the Christ, the Son of God, who is coming into the world."

Then they go near the tomb to find Mary weeping along with the Jews who were with her. Jesus' response—despite his power, majesty, divinity—he "was deeply moved in His spirit and greatly troubled."

"Jesus wept."

In doing so, Jesus' compassion connected with his dear friends, Mary and Martha, in their mourning, but he also connected with some of the Jews who witnessed this. They noticed, "See how he loved him." Jesus didn't *hocus-pocus-poof* in a manner of pride and power. He joined them—heart, soul, mind, and strength. He loved his neighbor as himself both in his humanity and his divinity.

Are we really looking for the glory of God? Do we recognize his steadfast love in the moments we're not getting the resurrection-and-the-life vibe?

If we see a glimpse of him, are we willing to also declare his consistent character by returning praise to him?

Maybe we think we are, but maybe we're looking for instant relief?

Maybe we're looking to political patches, feel-good feelings, humanitarian handouts, work ethic accolades, athletic honor, academic prestige, or anything less than the resurrection and the life.

In Acts 3:18-21, Peter reminds us, "But what God foretold by the mouth of all the prophets, that his Christ would suffer, he thus fulfilled. Repent therefore, and turn back, that your sins may be blotted out, that times of refreshing may come from the presence of the Lord, and that he may sent the Christ appointed for you, Jesus, whom heaven must receive until the time for restoring all the things which God spoke by the mouth of his holy prophets long ago."

Remembering back through this grief journey, mourning Jamie's loss, I confess several seasons where I withheld thanksgiving from the Lord. Honestly, I even squinted my jaws and locked my soul's scowl in place, containing trust to a controllable region of my heart and mind. Like Peter, I kept my eyes on the wind—and the sinking soul, my mind and my mire.

Part of this may have stemmed out of a misconception. Holiness and hope don't necessarily equate to jolly, persistent happiness, which is contingent on favorable circumstances and stirring fuzzy feelings. Rather, joy is a fruit of the Spirit seeding contentment deep into our souls and stirs encouragement soul to soul, despite circumstances.

I know now I've withheld full praise until I see what I want to see as a solution instead of remembering his character far surpasses my understanding. His purifying touch inhabits us in beautiful, powerful ways as we praise him in the process, step by step.

In regards to this project in particular, I did not want to share until I felt strong enough. I didn't want weakness. I didn't want pity. He's used both to teach me what compassion really is.

We're told to expect trouble in this world, but live in the knowledge Jesus has overcome, and he overcomes. We're told to "take up our cross daily and follow," not to illustrate ease, prowess, or even ethic but to obey and honor the divine dignity bestowed upon those who know only One is always holding us up. The One who chooses the foolish things of the world to tame the wise was born in a stable. His earthly character built up his heavenly witness to his father and perfect obedience to the mission.

Yet, we waver, whether with doubts like Peter or in our grieving ... we wander.

However, as I've submitted my weakness, fears, and rejections back to him, he's beyond faithful stirring life, light, and hope beyond all I can imagine. He does this still, but he especially did this in those early, dark hours of grief and loss.

Consider and answer me, O LORD, my God; light up my eyes, lest I sleep the sleep of death, lest my enemy say, "I have prevailed over him," lest my foes rejoice because I am shaken. But I have trusted in your steadfast love; my heart shall rejoice in your salvation. I will sing to the LORD because he has dealt bountifully with me.
Psalm 13:3-6 (ESV)

As if in darkness and shadows, we finally hear heaven's choir on horizons. What do we do next? We let the song swell and embrace us with deep discernment and delight.

"Holy, holy, holy is the Lord God Almighty, who was and is and is to come!"
Revelation 4:8

Refresh in the presence of the Lord. Rejoice! And remember his faithfulness. Remind one another who he was and is and is to come.

In the contrasting times of our earthly existence, we're reminded again and again who we are and who he is. Circumstances and loss wreak havoc on our emotions; however, they don't have to derail his character in us. Rather, when the winds and waves conspire, we ought to receive his reach to us, and we ought to extend his reach to one another.

Faith. Hope. Love. He is the only one always holding somebody up.

Worthy is the Lamb who was slain, to receive power and wealth
and wisdom and might and honor and glory and blessing! ...
To him who sits on the throne and to the Lamb be blessing
and honor and glory and might forever and ever!"
Revelation 5:12-13

"Let us pray: 'Thank you, Lord Jesus, that we know you are here, today—for us. ... Thank you that you came into the world as a Light, so that whoever believes in you does not remain in darkness. Make us joyful about that, so that we can be lights in this dark world, wherever you call us to be. Hallelujah! Thank you, Lord Jesus. Amen.'"
Corrie ten Boom
Messages of God's Abundance

As my dad (Jamie's Uncle Tim) said, "I think of the unparalleled joy of heaven, the unending purest kind."

"Put your hope in the LORD both now and forevermore."
Psalm 131:3

"Let us go to his dwelling place, let us worship at his footstool,
saying, 'Arise, LORD, and come to your resting place,
you and the ark of your might. May your priests be clothed
with your righteousness; may your faithful people sing for joy.'"
Psalm 132:7-9

setting sun

For years, I cringed when people said, "Life goes on." The cliché carried a nonchalance wrought with a numbing movement to limp on. But life does go on—Jamie's and ours.

Yes, memories still sneak into the present from time to time, and I remember well.

As mourning morphs into memories, shadows and absence still weigh in with waves of surprise and intensity. Rather than weighing in memories, Scripture-searching tears and listening prayers, I'm learning to pause, to invite and welcome grace to allow time to carry my gaze to God's goodness and faithfulness, pulsing life breath daily.

Sometimes, in the looking back he reveals his presence afresh. What the shadow of death haunts to hide, the shelter of the Almighty tenderly pulls close and teaches me to abide beyond the tears and fears.

Remembering One Rainy Drive

In the summer of 1991, just months before he died, Jamie and I were a couple of teenagers driving through a blinding, curving, slippery, hilly Oklahoma summer thunderstorm.

With the sun slipping beyond the hills and trees, lightning flashing all around, and thunder shaking the car I was driving, I nearly panicked. The road disappearing in the puddles, the tires tugging and churning, the spattering rain on the windshield—all inundating my sanity.

We had just spent a couple early evening hours hanging out with other teens we'd met through my church youth group. We underestimated the clouds' pace and the rains to come as they crowded out the sun. My fear of running late coupled with Jamie's relief to leave these strangers led us to hop away in a hurry.

Though we lived 700 miles apart, we stayed in contact through letters and phone calls. Then, every summer, Jamie's family sent him to spend time with my parents and me, days together riddled with ordinary rhythms and sibling-sounding banter.

We attended large public high schools. Since his freshman year, he'd been battling disappointment after disappointment. He always had the big dreams, the step-by-step strategy figured out, and the fortitude to overcome challenges. Like many from our era, he dreamed of flying fighter jets via the Air Force Academy—and eventually at Top Gun and in combat. In the meantime, football served as the training ground. Saturday's autumn allegiance was granted to the Nebraska Cornhuskers. Sundays filled first with church in the morning, but the afternoon's rest rang with the Denver Bronco games. Jamie never tired of watching, strategizing, and then, of course, running outside to "coach" and practice with his younger brother and any mildly willing neighbor friends. That is, until Hinckley High.

Instead of tryouts, they simply signed up for football, even as freshman. A game Jamie anticipated playing for years became a place and time of personal pain and unraveling destruction. We'll never know all Jamie endured as he watched his dreams of playing high school ball dissolve into a crass and cruel heap on the field by coaches—and the follow-up tormenting in the locker room by teammates.

My middle school years had been rough ones. After moving from a rural Wyoming town of 1,000 people to Tulsa—and nearly 1,000 people in my middle school—I found myself in rural-versus-city culture shock. From fashion styles to class sizes to "knowing my place" in a small community to "learning my place" in a larger one, at least basketball ought to be a familiar place for me to settle in. It was my sport of choice at the time.

However, can you even believe six-man basketball was what girls were still playing when I moved to Tulsa in the late 1980s? I played recreation league five-man for a couple years before moving, and I loved basketball. Sprinting down the court, dribbling through the legs, and swishing buckets. Competing as hard as I could against my hardy athletic peers in Wyoming.

In Oklahoma, I tried the six-man version. Three offensive players stay on one side of the half-court line and only play offense, while three defensive players defend the goal only on their side. It nearly killed my love for the game. Somehow, I'm not even sure of the details now, my mom signed me up for a dance team with an amazingly talented dance teacher who also happened to see potential in me ... me, the tomboy from Wyoming.

Dance spoke a physical language I learned and loved. I possessed just enough flexibility and determination to overcome my memory lapses and awkward angst against spandex and sequins. Through a rather quick succession of events, I accepted a special invitation to join a tryout competition squad. To my surprise, I made the cut. This led to dancing for a competitive school team in middle school as well as on a freshman competitive team and making the varsity dancing team with only two other sophomores. Honestly, I was never one of the best dancers on any of the teams I was honored to dance with. I can say, however, some people approach dance to execute the eight-counts or maybe simply to be seen, but I danced from the heart. I preferred practices to performances because I loved dancing for the joy of dancing—and team-building, the absolute best part.

All this to say, my high school experiences seemed to be widening my dreams and confidence ... as Jamie's seemed to be waning.

Yet, driving through that storm, my sanity shaky as my steering, Jamie spoke calmly, quietly, and even confidently:

"We're fine, Heidi. Just keep the car tight between the lines. Brake easy."

"We're alright. Drive as slow as you need. The storm'll pass."

"You're doing great. We're fine. We're almost home."

Mile by mile, his patient and persistent reassurance always calmed me.

Sure, I probably blabbed and blubbered on, spewing my doubts, but his outer calm often balmed my inner chaos. And he was right that night. We were fine. We made it home.

> "Who knows what the 'the communion of saints' means, but surely it means more than just that we are all of us haunted by ghosts because they are not ghosts, these people we once knew, not just echoes of voices that have years since ceased to speak, but saints in the sense that through them something of the power and richness of life itself not only touched us once long ago, but continues to touch us."
> **Frederick Buechner**
> *The Sacred Journey*

In the decades since, I cannot begin to count how many times the rainy roads scare and his calming words echo clear balms, even in his absence. One such instance was the year our eldest son turned 17 years old. I didn't want to think a mere number could trigger a year of fears. I happened to be at the beginning of a couple-year-long health battle, so I was physically weakening when the emotional eruption brewed deep below. As his primary home educator, I harbored fears for years of failing him and our other children. Yet, in these very months, I heard the words over and over again, "We're alright. We're almost home."

Being a mom and home educator has taught me much and convicted me often about the desire for home, the deficiencies of our earthly homes, and hope-yearning of a Heaven Home one day. As an imaginative child, I used to think heaven would be one vast wheat field on a perfect weather day with the smell of rain present, but not a cloud in the sky. Heaven felt real, but real far off, too. I think when people die, heaven hovers near the living, providing an embrace of present peace and a horizon of hope for eternity.

Stepping Steady

Another memory surfaces from sometime in late 1970s. ...

My parents often made play dates. However, today is not one of those days. This particularly ordinary day dawns with chores calling. Dad's working around the homestead as bread-baking occupies Mom in the kitchen. On such occasions, they send me outside after eating a hot homemade breakfast (usually bacon and eggs, pancakes, or oatmeal served with milk and orange or grape juice) until cold-cut lunch (on homemade bread) is served. Then outside again until the evening cool beckons more clothes or daylight disappears—whichever comes first.

While I don't recall Dad's full agenda for this day, I can still see him motioning to me, his four-year-old feisty princess. Wearing his worn work jeans, leather belt with buckle, and his dusty creased cowboy boots, he waves his glove bidding me to come.

My initial itinerary—to board the family boat parked next to the fence presently sunning canvas cover free, demanding I sail beyond the plowed horizon—immediately clears at my dad's invitation. Pretend play can wait. Dad needs a helper. Skipping to him as fast as my knobby-knees will carry me, I notice the old wooden ladder propped up against the west side of the barn.

"Heidi, climb on up!" he says as he points up the ladder.

Now, this is not the first time I'd seen a ladder or even climbed one. We often checked for damaged shingles after hail storms. But this ladder isn't resting against the side of the single-story ranch house. Something within me stirs.

"How far are we gonna go, Dad?"

Before he can answer, I grab on to begin the climb.

"All the way," he replies, holding the ladder sturdy before following me.

Hand over hand, step by step, rung by rung, I reach the top of the ladder only to discover just how much higher this old barn towers over the land. The sides float, only slightly higher than the house, while the center section seems to flirt with the clouds and winds.

As my feet propel the rungs under foot, my brow tightens, "Um, Dad, are you sure we can go to the top? Maybe just a little way up?"

His reply: "Ah, come on! You can do it! I am right here."

Despite his reassurance, hesitation mounts within me as I side-step off the ladder onto the green shingles of the old barn. I notice the Wyoming breeze pressing against my face and chest as I attempt to stand upright. Peering to my left, I see the freshly plowed field. Slowly, apprehensively, I squint to the right where the house squats.

As Dad dismounts, he says, "Go on up, Heidi."

As my childish legs slowly lead the way, the whisper inside grows louder. *"Ok, I'll venture to the middle of this hill, but I'm NOT climbing to the top!"* Seriously, the steepest section looks like a playground slide. Surely such an attempt will result in a slipping disaster like sledding off a cliff.

The hesitation swallows me as we reach the end of this set of shingles. The incline steepens. Walking upright is no longer an option. I entertain a timid contentment. We made it this far—far enough. For me, but not for my dad. He embarks on the next section propping himself up like one might push out of a swimming pool.

Dad demonstrates and says, "Take it one steady step at a time. Step with your feet. Steady with your hands. Step. Steady. Step. Steady."

Then, he quickens his pace to the top with ease of mind and lightness in his carriage. As he smiles down, his tenderness remains. Continually he calls, "Wait till you see the view from up here, Heidi! Nothing like it!"

The sandy-textured shingles beg my delicate hands to flee. As the doubts, fear, and loneliness linger with resounding clamors, questions race within my mind. Do I reject his calling? Is avoiding these piercing feelings an option? How can I control this situation? Where can I hide?

The sun beams down on me in a blink as the clouds continue racing overhead. In a moment of delicate stillness, my response speaks. Step by slow step, trembling ... sipping on the breath, "How can I doubt my dad?" He's calling. Time and again, he's led me on adventures to overcome my fears. Every time, despite the difficulty, gratefulness overflows. Not because the journey's easy, but because he leads me to the glory yet to be.

Over a decade later, when the fiercest tsunami of confusion suddenly summons me to the whirl of devastating grief, the realization beyond my darkest fears pricks every ounce of my being like a frenzied school of piranha. Dissimilar to joyful biddings, this pirate offers a sinister welcome to me, the brilliant wonder of life nearly severed and spoiled after Jamie's death by suicide.

He had roamed this land with me. Together, we'd gathered a satchel of memories. Together, we'd dreamed of growing up. Determined, we'd vowed to make the world a better, fairer place. All of this suffocated in a moment. I squeeze my eyes shut and hold my breath as the shards of questions berate me. Minutes, days, weeks, months march past. The previously predictable precision vanishes.

The coma of loss haunts and tempts me to linger. *"Don't look up! Stay right here. Don't trust the voice calling you to the spectacular view. Feeling joy will only heighten the depth of pain you're bound to endure again. Don't go. Think of the risk. You might slide right off the cliff with the storms that are bound to come."*

Yet again, the mysterious compassion and intervention of the Abba Father beckons me to step off the ladder of my selfish ambition and vain conceit. He calls me, step by step, to climb higher, listening to his voice. "Put your hope in the LORD both now and forevermore" (Psalm 131:3). Against the elements of doubt, fear, and loneliness hailing down, some steps seem to glide beneath me while others threaten to devour me. Still others, so mystifying, I cannot recall any details ... but teetering, I turn to look. His emboldening words bid my self-will to submit to him when all within me boils to fight in bitterness or to tuck and hide. Simply, his whisper, beyond the clamor of my own emotions, persuades muscles to respond one at a time. Higher and higher, all while becoming less about the height, more about the process.

Step. Steady. Step. Steady. Step.

The perspective from the peaks of grief calls me to the cross. My savior suffered an agonizing, humiliating death. Difficulty beyond comprehension is elemental to who he is and why he acts as he does. But defeat wilted with his glorious resurrection. He reigns. He composes murals and symphonies to restore beauty from ashes, stroke by stroke and note by note.

Funny thing about growing up, the process reveals I am not alone. Remembering to join the ancients' song in Psalm 133:1, "How good and pleasant it is when God's people live together in unity." And history's hum, "Nothing is new under the sun." While melancholy tones of self-protection track me still, his faithful majesty in the midst of my humanness bids still, step by step. *"How can I doubt my dad?"* When he calls me into the overwhelming, the uncomfortable, or even the mundane, he also mysteriously shines hope for the glory yet to be.

> *... the LORD bestows his blessing, even life forevermore.*
> **Psalm 133:3b**

Shadow of Absence ... Shelter of the Almighty

Shadows of absence and darkness drive weathering rains, but the climate is regulated by our refuge: he who provides in the shelter of the Almighty. Haunting me still? Sometimes. The testimony of four generations of family, God's word, and his creation revive and refresh the wonder of who he is and who I am in light of him. And what a gift we get to pulse out some of our precious hours together. He chooses to use seeing people among us to encourage and lighten our loads. Let's remember to thank him and thank them, even if the words don't come for decades.

And God chooses to use us, too. Sometimes, we see ... but choose to look the other way. When we hear whispers to reach out, no matter how simple, let's heed and act. We never know exactly how he chooses to illuminate light and breathe life again through our simple acts of obedience—including sharing our keen eyes of his hand among us.

> *That day, our epic of hope began ... even as death dawned*
> *a shrouding darkness on my family. Not an accident.*
> *Not an elderly relative ... not even a fit of rage. Rather, a seventeen-*
> *year-old young man silenced and stilled his own heartbeat.*

As decades dim the details of his death by suicide, we miss him still. With Michael, we echo, "I am glad he was my brother." With Uncle Carlton, we recognize, "Jamie's gone." Our days, our minutes with our people are passing. Sometimes we hurt hard when they go. With my Dad (Uncle Tim), we ask, "Under whose wing do I find my refuge and abide?" And beyond our own losses, compassion and comfort flicker and beam strong as abiding light. Even amongst climbs, steps, and shadows, a Heaven Home beckons us on, and we can still pray and rise, see and sing.

I waited patiently for the LORD; He inclined to me and heard my cry. He drew me up from the pit of destruction, out of the miry bog, and set my feet upon a rock, making my steps secure. He put a new song in my mouth, a song of praise to our God. Many will see and fear, and put their trust in the LORD. ... As for you, O LORD, you will not restrain your mercy from me; your steadfast love will forever preserve me!
David, Psalm 40:1-3, 11 (ESV)

Remembering to Remember

People ... are precious. Remind each other. Often. With courage and creativity.

Our times ... are temporary. Make memories. Especially at home. Gathering generations. Fuel fun, of course, but also circle up conversations uncovering the hard and the hurt with faith and prayer.

Hope ever hovers on the horizon ... deep calling deep. Seek to see the setting sun. Light leads us to linger and to love. When death and darkness thunder in too close, pause to feel the weight of the shadows among us—feel to lament, to grieve, to mourn, and ultimately ... to find refuge and to share compassion and care under the shelter of his wing.

Praise the LORD, all you servants of the LORD who minister by night in the house of the LORD. Lift up your hands in the

*sanctuary and praise the LORD. May the LORD bless you from
Zion, he who is the Maker of heaven and earth.*
Psalm 134:1-3

Resources

Continue the journey at **heidipaulec.com** for more encouraging resources, including discussion guides and thoughtful ways to share your stories. Connection can grow compassion and healing within grief.

If you or someone you know is struggling, reach out to my friends at RemedyLIVE.

RemedyLIVE.com
Text 494949 to access 24-hour chat center.

Or call the National Suicide Prevention Lifeline at 800-273-8255

About the Author

Heidi L. Paulec is an author and speaker with fifteen years teaching experience. She holds a bachelor's degree from John Brown University and a certificate of distinction from RZIM Academy. She has contributed to B1Studies with "Brave Girls Gather" and "Sacred Holidays" Bible studies .

She knows wounds, wandering, and wrestling serve as invitations to intimacy with God. Walking with Him, she's learning to discover ... to remember ... to share the beauty and wonder.

She and her family make their home in southwest Florida. She is a wife, a mom to three children, and an heir to sunrises and fresh-air adventures.